Register Now
to Yo

MW01074247

SPRINGER PUBLISHING COMPANY
C⃝NNECT™

Your print purchase of *Emdr Therapy and Mindfulness for Trauma-Focused Care,* **includes online access to the contents of your book**—increasing accessibility, portability, and searchability!

Access today at:

http://connect.springerpub.com/content/book/978-0-8261-4915-2 or scan the QR code at the right with your smartphone and enter the access code below.

UVEKVW5L

Scan here for quick access.

LS

SPRINGER PUBLISHING COMPANY

View all our products at springerpub.com

EMDR THERAPY AND MINDFULNESS FOR TRAUMA-FOCUSED CARE

ABOUT THE AUTHORS

Jamie Marich, PhD, LPCC-S, LICDC-CS, REAT, RMT, travels internationally to teach on eye movement desensitization and reprocessing (EMDR) therapy, trauma, addiction, expressive arts therapy, and mindfulness while maintaining a private practice in Warren, Ohio. Dr. Marich is the author of *EMDR Made Simple: 4 Approaches for Using EMDR With Every Client* (2011), *Trauma and the Twelve Steps: A Complete Guide to Enhancing Recovery* (2012), *Trauma Made Simple: Competencies in Assessment, Treatment, and Working With Survivors* (2014), and *Dancing Mindfulness: A Creative Path to Healing and Transformation* (2015). She is the founder of the Dancing Mindfulness practice and expressive-arts community and actively offers EMDR therapy training through her company, Mindful Ohio & The Institute for Creative Mindfulness. Marich began her career in human services as a civilian humanitarian aid worker in Bosnia-Herzegovina (2000–2003). Her award-winning dissertation research on the use of EMDR therapy in the treatment of addiction was published in two APA journals (*Psychology of Addictive Behaviors* and *Journal of Humanistic Psychology*). In 2015 she received the NALGAP President's Award for her work as an LGBT advocate.

Stephen Dansiger, PsyD, MFT, is clinical director of Refuge Recovery Centers in Los Angeles, a cutting-edge addictions treatment center where he developed and implemented the MET(T)A Method (Mindfulness and EMDR Treatment Template for Addictions). The treatment utilizes Buddhist psychology and EMDR therapy as the theoretical orientation and primary clinical practice. He is an EMDRIA Approved Consultant and Certified Therapist, and provides EMDR Basic Training and workshops through Mindful Ohio & The Institute for Creative Mindfulness. He is the author of *Clinical Dharma: A Path for Healers and Helpers* (2016) and avidly blogs and podcasts on topics related to mental health, recovery, and mindfulness. Besides maintaining a private practice in Los Angeles, he travels nationally and internationally, speaking and teaching on Buddhist mindfulness, EMDR therapy, the MET(T)A Method, trauma, the Refuge Recovery treatment model, and clinician self-care. He has been practicing Buddhist mindfulness for almost 30 years (including a one-year residency at a Zen monastery), and teaches dharma classes regularly at Against the Stream Buddhist Meditation Society in Los Angeles and at other centers nationally and internationally.

EMDR THERAPY AND MINDFULNESS FOR TRAUMA-FOCUSED CARE

JAMIE MARICH, PhD, LPCC-S, LICDC-CS, REAT, RMT
STEPHEN DANSIGER, PsyD, MFT

SPRINGER PUBLISHING COMPANY

Springer Publishing Company, LLC
11 West 42nd Street
New York, NY 10036
www.springerpub.com

Acquisitions Editor: Sheri W. Sussman
Compositor: S4Carlisle Publishing Services

ISBN: 978-0-8261-4914-5
ebook ISBN: 978-0-8261-4915-2

Downloadable Worksheets are available to all readers at springerpub.com/marich
Worksheets ISBN: 978-0-8261-4909-1

17 18 19 20 21 / 5 4 3 2 1

The author and the publisher of this work have made every effort to use sources believed to be reliable to provide information that is accurate and compatible with the standards generally accepted at the time of publication. The author and publisher shall not be liable for any special, consequential, or exemplary damages resulting, in whole or in part, from the readers' use of, or reliance on, the information contained in this book. The publisher has no responsibility for the persistence or accuracy of URLs for external or third-party internet websites referred to in this publication and does not guarantee that any content on such websites is, or will remain, accurate or appropriate.

Library of Congress Cataloging-in-Publication Data

Names: Marich, Jamie, author. | Dansiger, Stephen, author.
Title: EMDR therapy and mindfulness for trauma-focused care / Jamie Marich and Stephen Dansiger.
Description: New York : Springer Publishing Company, [2018] | Includes bibliographical references and index.
Identifiers: LCCN 2017037535| ISBN 9780826149145 | ISBN 9780826149152 (e-book)
Subjects: | MESH: Stress Disorders, Traumatic--therapy | Eye Movement Desensitization Reprocessing--methods | Mindfulness--methods
Classification: LCC RC489.E98 | NLM WM 172.5 | DDC 616.85/210651--dc23 LC record available at https://lccn.loc.gov/2017037535

Printed in the United States of America.

With love and gratitude to Joe Long (1980–2016), my friend and my "coach." You left us much too young and I will do my best, dear buddy, to continue writing from our shared mission of authenticity. Thanks for being my spiritual bouncer in this process!

—Jamie

With love and a deep bow to Maggie Estep (1963–2014). Thank you for helping me find my recovery, and then renewing my first-ever bilateral toolkit, my drumming. Every day that I help others stems directly from your reaching out all those years ago. And to Sadie, who keeps me in a steady gait toward true north . . . and to all the other Buddhas and Bodhisattvas I have met along the way.

—Steve

Contents

List of Meditation Practices and Experiential Exercises

Chapter 3

Mindfulness of Breath/Sensory Grounding
Mindfulness of Feeling Tone
Mindfulness of Mind
Mindfulness of Dharmas/Loving Kindness Meditation
Walking Meditation
Beginner's Mind Practice

Chapter 4

Diaphragmatic Breathing (Belly Breathing)
Complete Breathing (Three-Part or Dirgha Breathing)
Ujjayi Breathing (Ocean-Sounding Victory Breath)
Lion Breathing
Alternate Nostril Breathing (Nadhi Shodnan Pranayama)
Clench and Release: A Modified Progressive Muscle Relaxation Experience
Transforming Day-to-Day Activities into Meditation
Energetic Massage
Noodling: The Art of "Going With" Organic, Expressive Movement
The Expressive Arts as Meditation

Chapter 6

Demonstrating Hyperarousal and Release
Light Stream Multisensory Visualization Exercise
Tree Grounding Visualization Exercise
Simple Container Visualization Exercise

Foreword

EMDR therapy is the Dharma. Dharma means to see clearly and respond wisely. The Buddha often said that he only taught the truth of suffering and how to end suffering. Buddhism teaches many different techniques in the service of ending suffering, mindfulness being the main meditative technique offered in the core teachings, called the Eightfold Path.

EMDR therapy is mindfulness. Mindfulness is the Dharma.

When I learned that the core philosophy of EMDR is about bringing mindfulness to the held memories and sensations of our past traumas, while practicing bilateral attention, I realized that for the last 30 years, one of the primary practices I have been engaging in as part of my Buddhist training is walking mindfulness meditation. While walking slowly, bringing attention bilaterally, left-right, left-right to the sensations of each footstep. In the silence of retreat the mind often releasing the pain of the past. As I noted, right-left, right left. I believe that much of my early life suffering and trauma was reprocessed and integrated as the mindfulness of what was arising and passing was noted and eventually met with compassion and forgiveness.

When I told my father, Stephen Levine, about being trained in EMDR, he told me that Francine Shapiro had been his student around the time she had created EMDR and that much of it may have come from the mindfulness he was guiding her in as a way to be with grief.

As a Buddhist teacher, I believe that the Dharma (mindfulness being an integral part but not the whole of the Dharma) can alleviate all forms of suffering. Of course the end of suffering does not mean the end of pain or painful memories, it just means that we learn to meet our pain—physical, emotional, and mental—with understanding and compassion.

My training in psychology has shown me that without an embodied mindfulness component, conventional talk therapy has severe limitations. This is why I feel that the work that Dansiger and Marich are doing to move forward the great and skillful work of Shapiro is timely and necessary.

At Refuge Recovery Center, we train all our clinicians in EMDR therapy and the Refuge Recovery Buddhist approach to recovery. We have had great success helping our clients resolve the underlying trauma that led to their addictions, and so many of them have gone on to live happy and successful lives of abstinence and recovery.

I truly believe that the practice and philosophy outlined in this book have the power and potential to end suffering. This is revolutionary wisdom. We are on the front lines. The old guard has become complacent. Now is the time to move forward, to advance, to overthrow the causes of suffering.

Noah Levine, MA
Author of *Refuge Recovery,*
Against the Stream,
Dharma Punx

Preface

Helping professionals often describe what we do as assisting clients in the process of retraining, or rewiring, their brains. Both mindfulness and eye movement desensitization and reprocessing (EMDR) therapy can assist in this process, ultimately bringing about healthier, more adaptive lives for the people we serve. The benefits of pure mindfulness practice are more likely to be experienced over time, as long as practice is engaged in consistently. Although EMDR therapy is not a quick fix and may not work as quickly for everyone as certain promoters would have you believe, it is a more expeditious process. For people who have positively experienced EMDR (including your authors), a constant reflection is that EMDR facilitates shifts in consciousness both rapidly and quickly. At least once a week, people (clients, students, readers, community members) share with us some variation of the following statement: "EMDR moved in a few sessions what I couldn't do in years of talk therapy."

JAMIE'S JOURNEY: EMDR THERAPY OFFERS A NEW SOLUTION

In 2004, I began my master's level clinical counseling internship at a residential hospital for children and adolescents. My initial intention was to work with young people because serving as an English teacher in postwar Bosnia-Herzegovina from 2001 to 2003 sparked my interest in the helping professions. A very wise American social worker mentored me while I was in Bosnia, helping me to identify how unhealed trauma impacted the lives of my students. Thus, when I became acquainted with standard-model mental health care in the United States during my internship, I was surprised to encounter so many children who carried diagnoses such as attention deficit disorder, operational defiant disorder, conduct disorder, and the ever-popular bipolar disorder.

"Why isn't anybody looking at trauma?" I asked.

Some variation of, "We're not set up for that," was the usual response.

These responses triggered the parts of me naturally inclined toward fairness and justice. I found it very difficult to stay present at my internship site. I also became highly disturbed by how the kids were treated by doctors, staff members, and even many members of child protective agencies who were entrusted to advocate for them.

As my dissociative "checking out" moments intensified, so did the concern of a counselor on the residential unit, a lovely man named Joel. He pointed out my dissociative tendencies and lovingly asked how I planned to address them.

I protested, "I don't see how more therapy is going to help. I know what the answers are; I know what I should be thinking, I know what I should be doing."

At that point, I was in a pretty standard talk-therapy course of treatment with the third counselor I'd seen in my lifetime, and I'd been working a 12-step recovery program for the better part of two years. I was also active in a church. I didn't know what else was left to "do." Joel suggested that I chat with a professor in my graduate program with whom I was especially close and ask her advice.

When I talked with this professor and explained the essence of my dilemma, she responded, "Go see Janet Thornton over in Boardman. She does all of the weird, outside-the-box stuff."

For the first time since getting sober I experienced a hopeful sense of relief, simply by hearing that there were other approaches to be tried. Following my assessment session with Janet Thornton, she handed me what I now know to be a standard-issue EMDR International Association (EMDRIA) brochure on EMDR therapy. She directly recommended EMDR as a course of treatment for me, the first time I would ever hear those four letters strung together. At the risk of cliché, the experience literally saved my life and later transformed it. My depressive tendencies were known to come with suicidal ideations, and the EMDR treatment—specifically working on my first target, "I'm not lovable"—finally allowed those ideations to lift. I was able to stay more focused at the internship site and felt sufficiently empowered to ask my program for a new internship site, which I secured for the next semester. Moreover, my sobriety felt stronger than ever.

What amazed me the most about EMDR therapy during this first experience was how insights would just pop out of nowhere. These insights helped me connect so many of the proverbial dots in my life, revealing a complete picture that I was unable to see before. For the first time I was able to accept, at the deepest levels of my heart, my body, and my soul, that I am fundamentally a loveable person full of positive qualities and traits. As a result of being silent and reflective on certain parts of my experiences as the stimulation moved back and forth (in my case, it was the tactile stimulation machine), I noticed how the whole puzzle started to come together. I experienced what I've been fortunate to hear many clients subsequently affirm about EMDR: *The process allowed what I knew to be true in my rational mind to finally make sense in my heart.*

STEPHEN'S JOURNEY: A MINDFUL REVELATION

I received my intern number and found a job at a residential addictions rehab, where the clinical director invited me to go into private practice under her supervision. I knew she had a reputation for working with very difficult cases in which complex trauma was a factor. At one point, when she was working on a particularly difficult case, she told me she would bring in an EMDR consultant to help her in using EMDR with the client. I had been assisting this client to develop Buddhist mindfulness practices, something I had been doing for myself and others for more than 15 years by that time. To help coordinate our care my supervisor invited me to sit in on the weekly phone consultation, and the language and protocols of trauma-informed and trauma-focused treatment were introduced to me. As I heard how difficulties were overcome by both the therapist and the client, I became increasingly convinced that I needed to be trained in this therapy. I also heard the deep connections between my mindfulness work and this strange and seemingly powerful therapy. When I heard that our consultant was going to be providing training through the EMDR Institute, I signed up.

At the training I had a mindfulness-based revelation. During a practicum where I was taking on the role of the client, my partner went through the protocol note for note as we had learned it, and I applied my mindfulness practice to the experience, taking "just notice" very seriously. In very simple steps and in short order, the emotional charge of something that had bothered me for a very long time decreased. When it resolved as a completed and installed target, I tried to gather back my energy to have a dialogue about it. All I could muster was a weak, "What did you just do to me?" We both laughed. My long-standing Buddhist mindfulness practice had been screwed in tightly with bilateral stimulation, and the results were remarkable.

Thus began my ongoing relationship with EMDR therapy. Since that day I have practiced it as my primary mode of therapy, always informed by and channeled through the spirit of my mindfulness training. Francine Shapiro's original protocol, combined with the mindful presence of the therapist, is a powerful treatment not just for posttraumatic stress disorder (PTSD) but for difficulties that do not become full-blown psychological disorders. It works on single-incident trauma as well as complex trauma when used competently and with necessary modifications or adjustments when the wound is deep and the symptoms are profound. The research is quite robust related to PTSD, and it is growing with other difficulties and diagnoses. My own anecdotal experience is one of deep respect for the ability of the brain to heal, to figuratively scab and scar, and to become more adaptive in its functioning, when I am willing to stay out of the way as much as possible.

Through EMDR therapy, the client becomes able to live a more adaptive life. The language of the adaptive versus maladaptive that Shapiro prefers is infinitely helpful. EMDR is neither *Eternal Sunshine of the Spotless Mind* nor is it trying to do what many beginning meditators believe is supposed to happen—to end all thinking activity. EMDR therapy and mindfulness both point us toward our true north. All the gunk and junk that was piled on top of us is cleared away, leaving our beautiful shining strength and resilience, our powerful internal resources, our connection to ourselves and others, our birthright as human beings. I have experienced it as a client; I have experienced it as a therapist; and I have witnessed the stories of countless practitioners and sufferers who tell similar tales. Each day that I continue as a mindfulness practitioner and teacher, and as an EMDR therapist, my sense of wonder about the human spirit grows, and I see many people find one or more of the Four Divine Abodes in their lives—loving kindness, compassion, appreciative joy, and equanimity. This, I believe, is the journey of mindfulness and EMDR.

As an aid to practitioners, the clinical worksheets shown in Chapter 5 and the Appendix have been made available as PDFs that can be completed digitally or printed as needed. To download this supplemental material, go to www.springerpub.com/marich.

Acknowledgments

Our clients, consultees, and trainees in EMDR therapy remain our greatest teachers as we develop our teaching voices within the EMDR community. It is to all of them that both of us extend our heartfelt gratitude and appreciation! Throughout the composition of this book, we have seen your faces and heard your voices many times, and we thank you for joining us in our collaborative learning process.

We also wish to collectively thank Dr. Francine Shapiro and her early team of leaders, who steadfastly developed what we now know as EMDR therapy in the face of much adversity and opposition. We both consider EMDR therapy to be a great healing gift of which the Buddha himself would have been a fan, vital to our planet in these times. To these historical pioneers and to those who came before us, we extend our appreciation and gratitude.

Special thanks are due to Sheri W. Sussman at Springer Publishing Company for her faith in this project and for helping us to bring it to fruition. We also extend our thanks to Mindy Chen and other members of the Springer team for their tireless devotion to producing quality materials that support EMDR therapists in their growth.

Jamie: I wish to thank the members of our training team at the Institute for Creative Mindfulness—Amber Stiles-Bodnar, my co-author Steve Dansiger, Monica O'Connell, Teresa Allen, Thomas Zimmerman, Sharon Saul, Irene Rodriguez, Suzanne Rutti, and many others who have assisted us in the early collaborations to get our curriculum off the ground. Your advice and council inspires much of my writing in this book! I also extend thanks to my team of mentors and teachers in EMDR therapy who taught me a variety of valuable lessons over the years as I've grown as a therapist in this modality. Special thanks go out to Dr. Howard Lipke, Sarah Gilman, Dr. Laurel Parnell, and the late Sue Evans. I also send love and appreciation to my EMDR friends and colleagues in Brazil—during a trip I made to your beautiful country in 2014 to teach on EMDR therapy and addiction, you helped me to reconnect with just how much I love EMDR. This trip inspired my renewed commitment to EMDR teaching and writing. *Obrigada a todos.*

Finally, I thank my support system that helps me to grow in the light of healing every day. To David Reiter, for supporting this work, and to our incredible sons, Brendan and Ethan—I thank you for your willingness to share me with the world and for teaching me transformative lessons about the power of love and acceptance. To my family of choice—those in my recovery circles and those in my *Dancing Mindfulness* and expressive-arts circle: You infuse my life with meaning, more and more each day, and I hope to continue paying tribute to you in this dance called life.

Steve: I would like to thank my co-author, friend, and colleague Jamie Marich for everything that has transpired ever since I sought her out and my life changed course. I also thank everyone else at the Institute for Creative Mindfulness, especially Amber Stiles-Bodnar for welcoming me so fully into the fold. My mentors and teachers in EMDR therapy have been many, but a special thank you to Andrew Leeds for his steady guidance, AJ Popky for his direct support of my work in addictions, and Susan Brown for her pioneering work in EMDR and addictions.

I also want to thank my Buddhist teachers and guides along the way: Michael Kink, for bringing me to my first retreat and maintaining our spiritual friendship ever since; Seigan Ed Glassing, for his 30 years of practice as a monk shared with me at every turn; and Dr. Angie Chen, all my Zen teachers, and currently my Vipassana colleagues and teachers, particularly Noah Levine. I also want to thank my fellows in the recovery community for their strength, their vulnerability, their integrity, and their unconditional love.

My wife Sabrina continues to prove to be the greatest teacher I have ever encountered, and our daughter Sadie has proven to be a beacon and wellspring of loving kindness practice in both directions. So much love and gratitude to my little family, and a deep bow of gratitude to my ancestors and extended family, particularly the late Harry Dansiger. I hope this book in some small way reflects and produces his spirit of *tikkun olam*—repair of the world through acts of kindness.

1

Introduction

SHIFTING FROM TRAUMA-INFORMED TO TRAUMA-FOCUSED

As recently as 20 years ago, if you were a clinician practicing either mindfulness-informed interventions or eye movement desensitization and reprocessing (EMDR) therapy, it is very likely that your colleagues might have branded you a bit "fringe." Even insults such as "new age-y," "out there," and "loopy" might have been used to describe your therapy practice. To mark how much the times have changed, if you are working with mindfulness-informed interventions or EMDR in your current clinical practice, the phrases used to describe you may have shifted to "cutting edge," "innovative," and "inspired." In some clinical settings that seek to identify as trauma-informed, learning about the basics of mindfulness practice and EMDR or similar therapies may be an expectation.

Although critics of mindfulness and EMDR in clinical settings still exist, it is fair to say that both approaches have commanded the attention and interest of the psychotherapeutic field. Every year since 2012, at least 500 peer-reviewed studies have been published about the utility of mindfulness practice in both the psychotherapeutic and medical professions. EMDR therapy, once dismissed as pseudoscientific witchcraft by many factions of the helping professions, is now on the Substance Abuse and Mental Health Service Administration's (SAMHSA) National Registry of Evidence-based Programs and Practices for the treatment of posttraumatic stress disorder (PTSD). The World Health Organization, in its 2013 practice guidelines for treating trauma, heralds EMDR therapy as one of its two preferred interventions for healing trauma, citing a plethora of both research and practice knowledge.

This book is a presentation of how the two practices—mindfulness and EMDR therapy—are powerfully paired and, as a result, create a new paradigm for the delivery of trauma-informed services. Mindfulness as a practice dates back 2,600 years to the historical Buddha—a Nepalese sage named Siddhartha Gautama, whose teachings formed the foundation for what we now know as Buddhism. Many scholars describe mindfulness as the heart of Buddhist meditation. Delving into various perspectives on mindfulness and their clinical utility is one of the aims of this book, and we address the meaning of mindfulness throughout the chapters.

For the purposes of this introduction, we offer a definition of mindfulness that is generally put forth as a consensus in the peer-reviewed literature: The self-regulation of attention to the conscious awareness of one's immediate experiences while adopting an attitude of curiosity, openness, and acceptance (Bishop et al., 2004). Mindfulness can be practiced in its most classic form—sitting meditation—or through the wide array of activities and practices that make up our daily lives as human beings.

In the late 1970s and early 1980s, Eastern practices such as mindfulness meditation and yoga began to influence a larger conversation around mind–body medicine. During the 1980s, Francine Shapiro ardently educated herself in such practices following a cancer diagnosis. Shapiro recalls, in a documentary on EMDR by Michael Burns (2011), that she devoured every seminar and training she could attend on mind–body healing. In this interview and in several of her books, she describes how she developed a curiosity about experimentation with the interplay between her mental and somatic processes during this journey. These self-experimentations eventually led her, as she took a walk in a park one day in 1987, to the serendipitous discovery that would become EMDR therapy.

As she recounts in several interviews (Burns, 2011; Donovan & Nalepinski, 1999; Spierings, 2009), some distressing thoughts emerged as she was walking—normally the types of thoughts you would have to deliberately engage or bring up. She noticed that her eyes began an oscillating motion and she sat down to take a break, allowing the process to simply flow without judgment. Later in the walk, when she brought up the same thoughts and beliefs about self, she reports that they no longer seemed as valid (Shapiro, 2001, 2013; Shapiro & Forrest, 1997). From this experimentation—which many of us who are knowledgeable about mindfulness view as meditative curiosity—flowed her initial trial-and-error sessions with colleagues and willing volunteers to develop what would become the first protocol for setting up EMDR sessions. In the early days of 1989, *The Journal of Traumatic Stress* published a randomized controlled study on EMDR's forerunner, EMD, or "eye movement desensitization" (Shapiro, 1989).

What began as a simple desensitization technique described in that study has evolved into a complete system of psychotherapy with a model (adaptive information processing), a method (the various protocols for how EMDR therapy is delivered), and distinct mechanisms of action. The exact mechanisms are largely described in theoretical terms at the time of this writing (Bergmann, 2010, 2012; Pagani, Hogberg, Fernandez, & Siracusano, 2014), but some of us have long posited that mindfulness is one of the key factors in its efficacy (Logie, 2014; Sun, Wu, & Chiu, 2004; Tzan-Fu & Nien-Mu, 2006; Van den Hout et al., 2011). This book references how certain features of the standard EMDR protocol and some of Shapiro's most classic lines, such as "go with that" and "just notice," are clear evidence of her early mind–body training steeped in mindful tradition. EMDR therapy is now one of the most researched therapies on the treatment of PTSD. In 2014, Dr. Shapiro officially requested that practitioners start referring to EMDR as *EMDR therapy* (just as we in the field refer to cognitive behavioral *therapy* or dialectical behavior *therapy*), honoring EMDR as a complete system for healing.

The mindfulness system of healing—a reflection of the Buddha's psychological wisdom—and EMDR therapy as a total approach to psychotherapy offer our helping professions a path to redefining the paradigm for trauma care. According to SAMHSA (2014), to be trauma-informed requires understanding trauma and developing an awareness of the impact it can have across settings, services, and populations. Being trauma-informed involves viewing trauma through ecological and cultural lenses and recognizing that context plays a significant role in how individuals perceive and process traumatic events, whether acute or chronic. While trauma-informed care is the buzz phrase in modern helping professions, this book goes a step further, as utilizing mindfulness and EMDR therapy moves us to embrace *trauma-focused* care as the standard for clinical practice.

While we accept the SAMHSA definition as to the *what* of trauma-informed care, this book presents a design for *how* to optimally translate this intention into workable, dynamic, clinical action. *Trauma-focused* care denotes action. This book shares with you a vision for bringing this action to life by offering clinicians a design for optimally integrating mindfulness practice and EMDR therapy into clinical practice. The mission is to present this design in as practical and as real world of a manner as possible, even as peer-reviewed literature and research are cited. For many helping professionals, learning about both mindfulness practices and EMDR therapy may start with lessons in simple techniques that you can fold into your existing therapy practice. You may not yet be sold on the idea of mindfulness and EMDR therapy as a complete system of care, but adopting such a position is not a prerequisite for using this book. You may simply be interested in scanning this book for some techniques, and we hope our book meets your needs in that area—especially the chapters that teach the fundamentals of mindfulness practice and its clinical applications. Through your personal process of exploring this book, you may be inspired to develop a mindfulness practice for yourself. This personal engagement may give you broader insight into redefining how professionals and changemakers deliver trauma-focused services.

This book is not intended to be a replacement for formal training in EMDR therapy; we do not recommend that you delve into the EMDR chapters of this book (Chapters 5–9) unless you are trained. If you know very little about EMDR or do not practice it, this book can serve as a solid orientation, where you can learn about EMDR therapy through mindfulness. Shapiro drew on many mindfulness principles in her development of EMDR therapy, and some insight into this history is provided throughout the various chapters. If the ideas in the book do come to resonate with you—especially the mission of framing EMDR therapy in the context of mindfulness practice—pursuing further training and finding a home as an EMDR therapist may be for you. If you are already trained in EMDR therapy, this book may bolster your enthusiasm as you become more cognizant of the mindfulness elements within EMDR. Enhancing your clinical competency in mindful practices may directly correspond to how you deliver EMDR therapy. Many trainees in EMDR therapy can grow frustrated with the approach if they have a trainer who overwhelms them with the technical elements of EMDR and sticks solely to the prescribed scripts. Although your authors, as trainers in a program approved by the EMDR International Association (EMDRIA), are far from opposed to learning the proper technique of delivering EMDR therapy, we do believe there is an art to practicing EMDR that can be cultivated by recognizing the similarities between mindfulness practices and EMDR therapy. In the chapters of this book that specifically focus on the eight phases of EMDR therapy as defined by Shapiro, you are offered suggestions on how to deliver the protocol in a more mindful fashion. Practicing EMDR in this way eliminates much of the fear experienced by the newly trained; it can also revitalize your enthusiasm for practicing EMDR therapy if you are a veteran.

WHAT TO EXPECT FROM THIS BOOK

We wrote this book based on a shared vision and passionate belief that integrating mindfulness practice and EMDR therapy can be a game changer in the delivery of trauma-focused services. The various chapters go into the specifics of how you, as a clinician, can implement the solutions for integration that excite us in our clinical practice. However, a major component of working with mindfulness as a system of healing is to make it personal to you. If you choose to simply read the exercises and strategies on mindfulness to your clients in session, you may develop a solid intellectual understanding of the material. But to derive the fullest possible benefit from the content, we encourage you to personally engage in the mindfulness practices that we offer. Even if you do not like all of them, consider what you can learn about distress tolerance and being in the world with discomfort through the practice of stepping outside of your comfort zone. Notice how engaging in the practices yourself and seeing how you can integrate them into your daily life will put you in a better position to share mindfulness practices with your clients, specifically in EMDR therapy.

Chapter 2 calls for a paradigm shift: approaching clinical care as *trauma-focused* instead of simply *trauma-informed*. To illustrate this shift, the chapter presents a series of blueprints for integrating mindfulness practice and EMDR therapy. Chapters 3 and 4 are focused on learning mindfulness practices within a larger system of mindfulness-inspired healing, with step-by-step instructions and practical insights for clinical implementation.

Chapter 3 addresses the practices that are typically viewed as more traditional or classic: sensory grounding, breath awareness, breathing meditation, body scanning, feeling tone meditation, labeling, walking meditation, and loving kindness meditation. Chapter 4 explores the notion that one does not have to be in total stillness to be practicing mindfulness, and presents ideas for integrating day-to-day activities, movements, the expressive arts, and creativity into the practice of mindfulness and teaching clients. As in Chapter 3, emphasis is placed on trauma-informed language and variations for clients. Specific practices include muscle clenching and releasing, making day-to-day activities into objects of meditation, movement practices, yogic breathing practices, and approaching the expressive arts (e.g., drawing, music making/listening, dance) with meditative intention.

Chapters 5 through 9 cover EMDR therapy, and are organized along Shapiro's eight phases. Chapter 5 provides suggestions for how clinicians can practice Phase 1, Client History, more mindfully and with respect to trauma-informed values. Although tools such as worksheets or chronological histories can assist in learning about client history, you will discover that these alone are not sufficient. Rather, building the therapeutic relationship, determining clients' goals for treatment, and seeking to understand their presenting issues within the context of their treatment history are all imperatives. Competently addressing these imperatives can result from implementing mindful attitudes and approaches. The content covered in this chapter is valuable to both clinicians trained in EMDR and to those without such formal training.

Chapter 6 posits that EMDR Phase 2, Preparation, must include training in mindfulness practice. Such training can allow clients to enhance their repertoire of coping skills, build internal resources, and widen their affective window of tolerance. Special attention is paid to the role that cultivating mindfulness practices can play in heightening a client's distress tolerance. Allowing for this practice in the Preparation phase will more likely allow for successful trauma reprocessing in the later phases of the protocol. Many practitioners of EMDR therapy have been trained only in a few guided imagery exercises, believing this is sufficient for Phase 2. The information offered in this chapter guides both seasoned EMDR therapists and those who are new to it in how they can deliver Phase 2 in a more trauma-informed manner by incorporating mindfulness practices. Casting a wider net, this chapter contends that regardless of your primary modality of clinical practice, incorporating mindfulness into the early part of your treatment (preparation/stabilization) will enhance your clinical efficacy.

Chapters 7 and 8 are is largely written for the clinician already practicing EMDR therapy, as these phases are focused on the active reprocessing of traumatic memories. We cover mindful approaches for acquiring negative and positive cognitions during Phase 3, Assessment. These chapters discuss how mindfulness practice can assist in therapist attunement during Phase 4, Desensitization, and Phase 5, Installation, as bilateral stimulation is applied. Additionally, strategies are highlighted for keeping clients safe during abreactions using mindfulness skills discussed throughout the book. The importance of breathing (on the part of both client and therapist) during these vital phases, including the use of breath as an EMDR interweave, is also emphasized. This chapter also seeks to foster further critical thinking about the overall use of mindfulness practices as interweaves. Phase 6, Body Scan, as an EMDR component is also discussed in the context of mindful body-scanning approaches highlighted in earlier chapters of the book.

Chapter 9 covers EMDR Phase 7, Closure. From the inception of EMDR, Shapiro emphasized the importance of safely closing sessions. This chapter explores how all clinicians can benefit from the practice of closure that is a vital part of the EMDR approach. We take it a step further, utilizing mindfulness strategies to refocus and reengage our attunement with the client's experience. Calling upon mindfulness practices developed in Phase 2, Preparation, will allow clients to leave the clinical setting in as safe a manner as possible. Suggestions for therapeutic homework within a combined mindfulness-EMDR framework are also made.

Chapter 9 also focuses on EMDR Phase 8, Reevaluation. A major component of Phase 8 is reevaluating Phase 1, Client History, and determining if any other memories initially explored will need to be reprocessed. Other issues may have surfaced, either in the client's life or in the course of reprocessing other targets, which require therapeutic attention. Mindfulness practices help clinicians to increase their flexibility and openness to moving with the flow of a client's treatment. This practice helps clinicians become more adept at trauma-informed treatment planning, and this chapter offers a wealth of strategies for how clinicians can become competent in this process.

Chapter 10 highlights the notion that without mindfulness practices, EMDR therapy may be incomplete. A major topic covered in this chapter is the importance of embracing mindfulness as a way of life. Also showcased are the experiences of other colleagues and leaders in the field (including a review of the literature) on the idea that practicing mindfulness enhances professional competency. This chapter also explores insights for developing practices under the guidance of teachers and supporting other therapists in their quest to develop as trauma-informed practitioners. We wrap up the book by issuing a call to redefine how we can better take care of ourselves and, in turn, the people that we serve. Answering such a call can lead to renewal both in our personal practices and within the psychotherapeutic professions.

At the end of each chapter, you will notice a set of three or four questions for reflection and personal practice. A major part of working with mindfulness practice as a system of healing is to make it personal to you. Engaging in some meditation, reflection, or journal writing on these questions may help you deepen that process. In the realm of trauma work and EMDR therapy, it can also be difficult to take a client further into personal introspection than you have gone yourself. Although engaging with these reflection questions is certainly optional, this practice can certainly help to make the material more relevant and likely to be internalized.

The historical Buddha was concerned with suffering and the end of suffering. Your authors believe that the Buddha would appreciate how EMDR therapy helps to end suffering or, at very least, reduce its impact. The Buddha was a psychologist; he used the medicine of his time to describe the path to liberation, or the end of suffering. EMDR therapy is another expression of this path. We are delighted that you are choosing to journey with us in this book to consider how the integration of ancient wisdom—mindfulness practice—and creative innovation—EMDR therapy—can have a profoundly healing impact on our world.

REFERENCES

Bergmann, U. (2010). EMDR's neurobiological mechanisms of action: A survey of 20 years of searching. *Journal of EMDR Research and Practice, 4*, 22–42.

Bergmann, U. (2012). *Neurobiological foundations for EMDR practice.* New York, NY: Springer Publishing.

Bishop, S. R., Lau, M., Shapiro, S., Carlson, L., Anderson, N. D., Carmody, J., & Devins, G. (2004). Mindfulness: A proposed operational definition. *Clinical Psychology: Science and Practice, 11*, 230–241.

Burns, M. (Producer, Director, & Writer). (2011). *EMDR: We either transform pain or transmit it* [Documentary]. United States: Michael Burns Films.

Donovan, F. (Producer), & Nalepinski, B. (Director). (1999). *EMDR: Looking through hemispheres* [Documentary]. United States: Fran Donovan Productions.

Logie, R. (2014). EMDR—More than just a therapy for PTSD? *The Psychologist: A Publication of the British Psychological Society, 27*(2), 512–516.

Pagani, M., Hogberg, G., Fernandez, I., & Siracusano, A. (2014). Corrélats de la thérapie EMDR en neuroimagerie fonctionnelle et structurelle: Un résumé critique des résultats récents [Correlates of EMDR therapy in functional and structural neuroimaging: A critical summary of recent findings]. *Journal of EMDR Practice and Research, 8*(2), 29E–40E.

Shapiro, F. (1989). Efficacy of the eye movement desensitization procedure in the treatment of traumatic memories. *Journal of Traumatic Stress, 2*, 199–223.

Shapiro, F. (2001). *Eye movement desensitization and reprocessing: Basic principles, protocols, and procedures* (2nd ed.). New York, NY: Guilford Press.

Shapiro, F. (2013). *Getting past your past: Take control of your life with self-help techniques from EMDR therapy.* Emmaus, PA: Rodale Books.

Shapiro, F., & Forrest, M. (1997). *EMDR: The breakthrough "eye movement" therapy for overcoming stress, anxiety, and trauma.* New York, NY: Basic Books.

Spierings, J. (Producer). (2009). *EMDR interview with Francine Shapiro* [YouTube clip]. Retrieved from https://www.youtube.com/watch?v=8GUd5hhnkVE

Substance Abuse and Mental Health Services Administration. (2014). *A treatment improvement protocol: Trauma-informed care in behavioral health services.* Washington, DC: Author.

Sun, T. F., Wu, C. K., & Chiu, N. M. (2004). Mindfulness meditation training combined with eye movement desensitization and reprocessing in psychotherapy of an elderly patient. *Chang Gung Medical Journal, 27*(6), 464–469.

Tzan-Fu, S., & Nien-Mu, C. (2006). Synergism between mindfulness meditation training, and eye movement desensitization and reprocessing in psychotherapy of social phobia. *Chang Gung Medical Journal, 29*(4), 1–4.

van den Hout, M. A., Engelhard, I. M., Beetsma, D., Slofstra, C., Hornsveld, H., Houtveen, J., & Leer, A. (2011, December). EMDR and mindfulness. Eye movements and attentional breathing tax working memory and reduce vividness and emotionality of aversive ideation. *Journal of Behavior Therapy and Experimental Psychiatry, 42*(4), 423–431.

2

Redefining the Paradigm for Trauma-Focused Care

A NEW HOPE

In redefining and establishing a new paradigm for services as trauma-focused, this book seeks to offer clinicians a grounded and mindfully present spirit of "both/and" rather than the divisive and limiting "either/or." This presents a number of hurdles from which many theorists, researchers, and practitioners might ordinarily shy away. The first hurdle is that of the scientific method and the belief that the more variables that are present (i.e., the more elements we are throwing into the kitchen sink), the less likely we are to be able to determine what is working or not working in our attempts to care for people. The second hurdle is that element of human nature that at times, either healthfully or pathologically, needs to take a stand, to plant a flag somewhere very specific, to state a case and have it provide meaning and structure. A third hurdle involves several manifestations of that either/or thinking: my way or the highway; I am right/you are wrong; it is this way/definitely not that way.

EYE MOVEMENT DESENSITIZATION AND REPROCESSING THERAPY

The first solution to catapult over these hurdles exists in the ever-changing, still-growing world of trauma theory. Trauma derives from the Greek word *traumatikos*, meaning "wound." In a broad, humanitarian sense, we define trauma as any unhealed human wound or series of wounds—physical, emotional, sexual, spiritual/existential, and financial/economic. The first appearance of a clinical diagnosis directly naming trauma—posttraumatic stress disorder (PTSD)—appeared in the *Diagnostic and Statistical Manual of Mental Disorders* (*DSM*) in 1980, long after the clinical world was already wrestling with trauma and its effects on human behavior (American Psychiatric Association, 1980). The definition of trauma stemmed less from the effects on the person than it did from the nature of the event. To be viewed as a trauma victim, an individual needed to experience an event that met criteria for a dedicated traumatic experience: "Criterion A trauma under the PTSD diagnosis." Many factions within the helping professions have since realized that the internal world of the sufferer has a great impact on how those who seek help need to be treated.

This subjectivity requires the "both/and" lens: Helping professionals need to consider the external events driving the response as well as the response itself. More importantly, we must look at the content and the extent of the internal experience. Dr. Francine Shapiro, the creator of eye movement desensitization and reprocessing (EMDR) therapy, played a visionary role in helping our clinical professions to acknowledge that unhealed trauma is a much broader issue than could be encapsulated by the simple *DSM* definition of PTSD. Her early presentations of "large-T" (i.e., PTSD-qualifying) and "small-t" trauma (i.e., everything else) (Shapiro, 1995) started an important conversation. In her updated presentation of the adaptive information processing (AIP) model, the collection of theoretical underpinnings supporting EMDR therapy, Shapiro posits:

> Trauma can include *DSM-5*® Criterion A events and/or the experience of neglect or abuse that undermines an individual's sense of self-worth, safety, ability to assume appropriate responsibility for self or other, or limits one's sense of control or choices. (EMDR International Association, 2015)

Whether or not you identify as an EMDR practitioner, adopting this general approach to trauma is critical in the modern era.

With this trauma-focused framework, helping professionals are able to conceptualize cases from a more client-centered perspective. Inherent in this approach is collaboration and the Rogerian notion of entering the client's world. Armed with knowledge of the complex nature of trauma and its effects, clinicians can meet clients where they are in their process of understanding and grappling with their difficulties, and more effectively facilitate a process of deeper understanding and integration. That integration comes not from creating a hierarchy of trauma and a list of events that qualify, but instead from a relationally mindful understanding of the impact of the past on the present and future adaptive functioning of the client.

Another helpful framework that has yet to make it into the *DSM* but has become mainstream in the trauma treatment world is the construct of Complex PTSD (Courtois & Ford, 2009; Herman, 1992). Abuse and neglect of many kinds can be carried out over time. Even single-incident traumas can have ripple effects that may be lost sight of in the assessment and treatment of the original identified trauma. We must be alert to the complications and specific manifestations of difficulties fed by ongoing external events and the internal reinforcement of those events. Now that clinicians are looking to treat as many traumatized people for as many symptoms of traumatization as we can—whether that trauma stems from a single incident or complex and repetitive events—we need to have a more nuanced view of the problem and the solution. These nuances are addressed in the growing literature on Complex PTSD and development of specialized protocols within EMDR therapy. A key to the both/and framework for trauma-focused care is to include the great work of theoreticians, researchers, and practitioners who have given years of attention to these matters.

Evidence of the second hurdle can be found in the history of turf wars within the field of psychology. These wars are by no means over, but significant progress toward settling them has been made by the folding of spiritual psychology, complementary medicine, East-meets-West interventions, and many other integrative strategies into the care of those suffering from mental and emotional difficulties. The literature on spiritual psychology and its role in mental health has grown significantly over the past 20 years (Hill & Pargament, 2008). Complementary medicine, including acupuncture, massage, and yoga, has entered the mainstreams of medicine and mental health treatment. The meeting of East and West has manifested in many quarters, most significantly in the advent of mainstreamed mindfulness therapies (Aich, 2013).

Even with these advances in the world of both/and, many practitioners and other experts continue to plant their flag on one side or the other. Such exclusionary mindsets are not unique to the scientist; those more squarely located on the spiritual side of the fence can become just as attached to their views. These stances are the last vestiges of the long battle between matters of the spirit and of science. Throughout the 20th century, and then amplified by the social media culture of the 21st century, many have claimed to have found "the answer." They have discovered the magic formula. The cure/ fix/panacea can be found in the form of a seven-item checklist in a blog post that went viral, with a TED Talk attached. Sometimes there is substance to be found, but the main object is too often the marketing of a brand.

Some of the greatest battles have been between those professing a medical model for treatment and those proposing a more psychosocial and/or spiritual approach. And while there has been great progress in bringing both sides to the negotiating table, there is certainly more work ahead. This book's emphasis on trauma-focused care hopes to be inclusive and integrative, generating a movement of our healing communities toward holistic solutions.

MINDFULNESS

This brings us to Buddhist mindfulness and EMDR therapy. The historical Buddha did not come up with a number of techniques designed to be helpful in difficult spots and used in a pinch. He devised a comprehensive system of psychology and spiritual practice that was the result of a long-running scientific experiment he performed on himself, 2,600 years ago, without the aid of brain-scanning equipment or randomized controlled studies. The Buddha chose to look inward and, from an objective viewpoint, deeply probe the nature of the mind—his mind. He used the technology of the day, most of which had been created by spiritual seekers and teachers in India, alongside a fully formed system of medicine, Ayurveda.

Siddhartha Gautama's first experiment came when, as a sheltered prince, he left the palace grounds where he had spent the 30-some years of his life. Outside those walls he found the reality of suffering in the forms of sickness, old age, and death, and was drawn to the monastic life. For the next several years, he traveled throughout India seeking teachers who could impart to him the wisdom and skills to calm the mind and to bring peace to himself and others. By this time he was a renowned ascetic, living in denial of the body with the goal of emboldening the spirit. It was then, as he sat beneath what would become the Bodhi tree, that he had his initial enlightenment experience—the recognition of the need for a Middle Path to healing, or an integration of the mind and the body. He arrived at his answer through a single-case study: through direct experience and direct observation, a scientific application of the mindfulness and concentration he had developed over more than a half-dozen years of inquiry (Batchelor, 2010). The Buddha did not immediately know how to explain this experience, and at first vowed to remain silent about it because he believed no one would understand it. When he finally tasked himself with teaching, he went to the science of the time to explain his system of psychology.

His model will look very familiar to the Western medical practitioner: a diagnosis is presented, the symptoms and causes are revealed, the cure is offered, and a prescription to enact the cure is designed. In the first of his Four Noble Truths, the Buddha provided a diagnosis of the core problem of life: suffering. The Second Truth speaks of the symptoms and causes of this suffering: Pain is a guarantee in this life, but suffering is caused by craving, clinging, aversion, and unhealthy attachment to material things, people, results, and experiences. Simply put, the problem lies not in the experience of pain but in our interpretation of it. He quickly provides the cure for this in the Third Truth: Get into and through these causes and conditions to end the suffering. And finally, the Fourth Truth lays out the Buddha's prescription—the Eightfold Path.

This prescription is a complete system that contains all the hallmarks of what modern helping professionals work with our clients to accomplish. We want them to grow in wisdom and self-understanding. We help them identify and deal with blocking beliefs so that they may set healthy intentions. We hope that they can speak, act, and work in ways that lead to continued growth and more skillful, adaptive ways of being (Bodhi, 2006).

The Buddha very clearly informed his adherents that he was not God. As to whether a God existed, he did not offer a definitive position. He was, however, definitive about his teaching: the end of suffering—a concept that could easily fit on the shingle of any psychotherapist's office or serve as a branded meme on social media. But consider his ultimate goal from a much deeper place: To truly conceptualize and internalize an end of suffering, it is important to understand what this system of healing entailed.

The most remarkable aspect of his approach at the time (and that remains so to this day) is his focus on mindfulness. One could say that the entire Eightfold Path described in the prescriptive Fourth Truth is ultimately about mindfulness. Breaking it down, one could hone in on the fact that the last three elements of the path—effort, mindfulness, and concentration— specifically address mindfulness meditation as central to his solution. What made the Buddha unique was his focus on mindfulness and concentration. Many meditation masters of the time used deep states of concentration to perform great spiritual, physical, and psychological feats. The Buddha, however, believed that these feats were primarily self-serving, and that an objective, mindful awareness of the reality of suffering and other inherent realities of life would provide a deeper, direct experience and result in physical, spiritual, ethical, and psychological wellness (Batchelor, 2010).

In his formulation, Buddha proposed that mindfulness, ethical living, and wisdom are intimately connected. Although the Eightfold Path is laid out as a list so that it may be read and understood, it might better be perceived as a wheel. Certainly, the path does not seem like a straight line most of the time, much like our own lives and the lives of our clients. However, "right understanding," the first element of the path, speaks to the need for at least enough wisdom to believe that following these steps might be a good idea. The second factor—"wise intention"—brings purpose and completion to wise thoughts (Bodhi, 2006).

Then we step into the three ethical factors of speech, action, and livelihood, where our clients (in their lives) and we (as practitioners) reap further wisdom and take opportunities to apply newfound mindfulness skills. In many modern formulations of mindfulness, the emphasis is on skills training rather than ethical factors. For our purposes, the successful application of mindfulness, as well as the reevaluation and future template work in Phase 8 of EMDR therapy, depends upon these real-world examples of how mindfulness can manifest in everyday life. The Buddha's conception was that if we are consistently attempting—through speech, action, and livelihood—to live mindfully in the world, we will create infinitely less suffering for ourselves and others. This creates a snowball effect: greater wisdom leads to better day-to-day living, which leads to a growing sense of peaceful and mindful awareness.

So now mindfulness has entered the mainstream of Western psychology. There are debates over its efficacy, its proper use, and the diagnoses for which mindfulness practice is indicated, but these are healthy discussions that bring the importance of mindfulness into clearer view. Mindfulness is a useful component of recovery from any number of ailments and injuries. This becomes evident upon examining the new landscape of mindfulness-based therapies, which include dialectical behavior therapy, mindfulness-based cognitive behavioral therapy, mindfulness-based stress reduction, and many other formulations either proposed, in development, or currently in use. Clinicians are using mindfulness at the center of treatments for such problems as depression, anxiety, PTSD, addiction, and personality disorders.

How does this holistic view of mindfulness synch so elegantly with EMDR therapy? The AIP model, the eight-phase protocol, and the three-pronged protocol (i.e., past–present–future orientation in clearing targets) also represent a complete system of psychology. Embedded within EMDR therapy are several elements addressed by mindfulness, including stabilization, grounding, resourcing, and the ability to toggle between somatic and cognitive experience. Helping the overly cognitive person to discover a somatic experience, or helping someone who cannot connect the body and the mind, are baseline needs for the trauma-focused therapist.

The original Phase 1 and Phase 2 toolkit designed by Shapiro for these needs was incredibly useful, if ultimately incomplete (Dworkin, 2005; Greenwald, 2007; Korn & Leeds, 2002). Many EMDR theorists and practitioners have filled gaps in Shapiro's work, adding or subtracting as necessary to meet needs of the complex client—those with dissociation or with fearful or dismissive attachment styles. The redefined paradigm for trauma-focused care proposed in this book suggests that Buddhist and other forms of mindfulness represent a complete system within EMDR therapy. Mindfulness allows a client to achieve the level of integration that will empower them to do trauma reprocessing and achieve the desired level of relief from symptoms and the resulting full integration of memories.

The feeling is mutual when the roles are reversed. EMDR therapy provides a missing piece to mindfulness in the context of treating the difficulties that are coming into our office in the 21st century. A story about the Fourteenth Dalai Lama is pertinent here. The Dalai Lama is a lover of science, with an infinite curiosity that has resulted in his creation of the Mind and Life Institute, which has hosted conferences on scientific subjects for more than 25 years. He has also written extensively on scientific topics. At one conference he asked a group of Western psychologists, "What are your most common presenting issues in treatment?" The clinicians got together and gave a group reply: "low self-esteem, even self-hatred." The Dalai Lama and his translator got into a spirited discussion, after which the Dalai Lama replied: "We don't have a word for this in Tibetan."

He went on to discuss some of the Buddhist mindfulness teachings regarding impermanence and the lack of a solid self that one can proclaim as the self at any given moment (Kornfield, 2010). That, and the fact that the ethical factors of the Eightfold Path look outward toward helping others as opposed to building the ego, leads to a lack of this self-hatred dilemma in a Buddhist culture, according to the Dalai Lama and others. The development of care and concern for others and for oneself as part of the larger human community is another element of this culture, a feeling of loving kindness and compassion that acts as a frontloaded antidote to ill will, including ill will toward self.

If a person of the 21st century who is not from a Buddhist upbringing attempts to develop a mindfulness practice without also addressing any attachment, developmental, or event-based traumas, that individual may not be able to easily enter or maintain the Eightfold Path. The Buddhist teaching of not-self does not resonate with or may even result in harm to someone who needs to build some ego strength to move more adaptively through life. EMDR therapy itself is a mindfulness practice for both clinician and client that results in the dedicated reprocessing of material that then allows for a more settled and comprehensive relationship with the classical mindfulness practices. With the advent of EMDR therapy, we have arrived at a place where people can heal from their difficulties in such a way that their wisdom is built, they can set wise intention, and they can live a more adaptive life as described by the Buddha. They can continue to build that life through continued mindfulness practice.

Buddhist mindfulness provides a great deal of the preparation required of the EMDR client, then trauma is reprocessed and future templates are installed using the remainder of the eight-phase protocol. Clients can provide their own aftercare with Buddhist psychology and mindfulness, or another mindfulness path that deepens the direct life experience of the practitioners. Again, Buddha taught suffering and the end of suffering. EMDR therapy has brought the end of a specific and exacerbated grade of suffering to hundreds of thousands of people over the past 25 years. It seems like it has become part of our Right Understanding, a path to a deeper wisdom, a path to a more adaptive life. This indeed is the framework for the new paradigm for healing.

THE FUSION OF MINDFULNESS AND EMDR THERAPY

Mindfulness can be defined as the practice of coming back to awareness. Defining mindfulness in this way becomes very useful in working with clients, especially those who believe that they can't meditate. Here is a short list of excuses that you may have heard from clients:

- "I can't sit still."
- "Meditating makes me more anxious."
- "Getting that quiet makes me nervous."
- "I'm a failure at doing it right."
- "I'm not really a spiritual person."
- "Meditating goes against my religion."

Many clients struggle with beginning to embrace meditation because of stereotypical, religiously charged images of mindfulness that abound, such as the shaven-headed Buddhist monk in robes on retreat. Images of the modern mindfulness movement—like sitting in a perfect cross-legged position beneath a tree on a beach while clad in trendy yoga clothing—are no better because they portray mindfulness as total peace, relaxation, and stillness. The reality of the practice is much more complex and rich: a sea of thoughts, images, emotions, and distractions will come at anyone who seeks to meditate or engage in other activities of daily living. The challenge is in learning how to stay present and aware with whatever life may bring—good, bad, or neutral. By regarding mindfulness as *the practice of coming back to awareness*, clinicians recognize that attention *will* drift and wander. Neither this wandering nor these reactions make one any less of a person. They make us human. Highlighting this reality for clients may help them shed some of their preconceived notions about mindfulness and meditation and feel more inspired to give the practice an honest attempt.

The modern world is rife with distractions and expectations that battle for our presence, attention, and focus. Mindful practice is not about making those distractions and triggers go away—they are always going to be there. To be a practitioner of mindfulness, neither client nor clinician need strive to be that Buddhist monk or that perfectly still meditator beneath a tree. We need simply to practice paying attention; practice bringing awareness back to the present moment when we notice that awareness is drifting. One of the gifts of mindfulness practice is that we can better recognize when our attention is wandering or when visceral responses are flaring up in the body. It is little wonder that mindfulness teachers explain the practice as exercising our metaphorical awareness muscle. The clinical value of such practices is obvious, particularly as clients prepare for EMDR therapy.

The English word *mindfulness* in the context of Buddhist practice was not coined until the 1800s. "Mindfulness" generally refers to both the Pali word *sati* (*sarati* in the verb form) and the Sanskrit term *smrti*. There are subtle nuances in the translations that can be noted and mined for clinical value. Arriving at an exact definition is not as important as considering some of these translational insights and recognizing those that may resonate with the individual. Clients and clinicians can recognize those resonances and let them enrich a personal practice. In addition to mindfulness as the practice of coming back to awareness, modern Theravadan Buddhist teacher Bhikku Bodhi's reflections on the limitations with the word *mindfulness* are significant:

The word derives from a verb, *sarati*, meaning "to remember," and occasionally in Pali *sati* is still explained in a way that connects it with the idea of memory. But when it is used in relation to meditation practice, we have no word in English that precisely captures what it refers to. An early translator cleverly drew upon the word mindfulness, which is not even in my dictionary. This has served its role admirably, but it does not preserve the connection with memory, sometimes needed to make sense of a passage. (Inquiring Mind, 2006)

Bodhi's observation, excerpted from a larger interview he gave on translating Buddhist teachings, suggests that the translation and what it means to practice can vary among practitioners and traditions. The role of memory in the very meaning of the practice is also of great importance. Consider how memory as an essence of mindfulness practice furnishes a golden link between mindfulness and EMDR therapy.

EMDR therapy allows for some talking and asking of questions, which can be important in human relations. However, the level of silence and introspection that the EMDR approach promotes is a major component of its effectiveness for so many people. This silence, generally experienced during the application of bilateral stimulation, allows clients to go within and simply notice internal experience, a process that allows them to arrive at their own insights and solutions instead of relying on the "expert" therapist to unveil the answers. The underlying assumption of EMDR therapy is that human suffering results from physiologically stored, unprocessed memories

(Shapiro, 2001; World Health Organization, 2013). The AIP model, which Shapiro presents as a framework for explaining EMDR, gives clinicians a road map for helping individuals alleviate their own suffering by reprocessing these memories. The methods and mechanisms that EMDR therapists learn to apply can facilitate this healing, and they are constantly learning new, more artful ways to use these skills within the context of the therapeutic relationship.

Many clinicians who arrive at EMDR trainings are looking for new ways to help their clients. They've learned that talking about traumatic experiences is not enough to bring about lasting change. Many report that they've been the *trauma champion* in their agencies or hospital settings for years, often ridiculed or scorned for wanting to focus on trauma in conceptualizing cases. In the EMDR approach to psychotherapy, such a trauma focus is not looked down upon; it is celebrated. "What role is trauma playing in this clinical presentation?" is the question that defines conceptualizing cases in the EMDR approach. With EMDR therapy, you are empowered with a set of skills to help clients reprocess traumatic memories and essentially heal themselves, reducing the impact of suffering in their own lives and in the lives of others around them.

EMDR therapists use classic phrases like "go with that" or "just notice that" as the bilateral stimulation is applied and the storage of traumatic memories moves and shifts. However, EMDR clinicians and clients may find themselves using these phrases in other aspects of living. EMDR therapists can actively encourage this process as they teach clients to carry the fruits of their therapeutic experiences into the arena of daily life. Consider Alex, a college student in her early 20s who presented for clinical services due to crippling anxiety. Alex noticed immediately through client history, preparation, and the first few sessions of reprocessing that her anxiety was clearly linked to obsessive thoughts about things and situations that would likely never play out. Through the mindfulness skills Alex's therapist taught in preparation and the practice of "just noticing" that Alex learned in EMDR therapy, she began to notice the first signs of obsession in day-to-day life. This early awareness became evident by noticing subtle distresses in the body. As she learned in the EMDR process, Alex continued to "just notice" the body level distress if it flared up, instead of stewing about it further or engaging in an unhealthy behavior like binge eating. Alex learned to notice it fully, without judgment, as she breathed. No specific use of bilateral stimulation or dual attention stimulus is needed in the context of life. Simply *noticing* can prove to be a helpful practice, in and of itself, for helping clients learn to deal with the stressors of daily life and build a greater sense of mind–body awareness.

TYING IT ALL TOGETHER

Mindfulness practice, as described in a classic metaphor by Jon Kabat-Zinn, can teach people how to surf when waves of stress and emotion come rolling in. Dr. Bessel van der Kolk (2014), an important figure in advancing scholarship on trauma, explains that mindfulness practice allows the executive brain to inhibit, organize, and modulate the hardwired automatic reactions preprogrammed into the emotional brain. In his landmark work, *The Body Keeps the Score: Memory and the Evolving Psychobiology of Posttraumatic Stress*, he summarizes the following benefits of this process for survivors of trauma:

- Traumatized people are often afraid of feeling—mindfulness practices can help orient them to and ease them into this process by widening sensory experience.

- Practicing mindfulness is calming to the sympathetic nervous system, lessening the destruction of fight/flight responses.

- The practices help to promote distress tolerance as awareness develops that emotional states constantly shift.

There is a treasure trove of information here for EMDR therapists. Why wouldn't we align these benefits into our practice of EMDR? There are so many natural combinations of these practices that can enhance the flow of EMDR therapy. By weaving mindfulness into the early phases of EMDR, we offer an enhanced experience for our clients, especially by widening their affective windows of tolerance, which is vital in the reprocessing phases of EMDR as we target the trauma. As we bring EMDR therapy to a close, we can discharge our clients with a wide set of mindfulness skills that they can continue to access after therapy formally terminates, skills that are vital for resilience and continual adaptation to the circumstances, stressors, and suffering that is the human experience.

QUESTIONS FOR REFLECTION AND PERSONAL PRACTICE

- What is my personal, working definition of mindfulness?

- How am I already practicing mindfulness in my daily life, even if I don't have a specific meditation practice?

- What are some of the similarities, links, and points of fusion I've already started to notice between mindfulness practice and EMDR therapy?

REFERENCES

Aich, T. K. (2013). Buddha philosophy and western psychology. *Indian Journal of Psychiatry,* *55*(Suppl. 2), S165–S170.

American Psychiatric Association. (1980). *Diagnostic and statistical manual of mental disorders* (3rd ed.). Washington, DC: Author.

Batchelor, M. (2010). *The spirit of the Buddha.* New Haven, CT: Yale University Press.

Bodhi, B. (2006). *The noble eightfold path: Way to the end of suffering.* Onalaska, WA: Pariyatti Press.

Courtois, C. A., & Ford, J. D. (2009). *Treating complex traumatic stress disorders: An evidence-based guide.* New York, NY: Guilford Press.

Dworkin, M. (2005). *EMDR and the relational imperative: The therapeutic relationship in EMDR treatment.* New York, NY: Brunner-Routledge.

EMDR International Association. (2015). *Basic training curriculum requirements.* Retrieved from http://c.ymcdn.com/sites/www.emdria.org/resource/resmgr/BasicTraining/BTCRequirements.pdf

Greenwald, R. (2007). *EMDR within a phase model of trauma-informed treatment.* New York, NY: Haworth Press.

Herman, J. L. (1992). *Trauma and recovery: The aftermath of violence—from domestic abuse to political terror.* New York, NY: Basic Books.

Hill, P., & Pargament, K. (2008). Advances in the conceptualization and measurement of religion and spirituality: Implications for physical and mental health research. *Psychology of Religion and Spirituality, Special*(1), 3–17.

Inquiring Mind. (2006, Spring). Translator for the Buddha: An interview with Bhikku Bodhi. Available online at http://www.inquiringmind.com/Articles/Translator.html

Korn, D., & Leeds, A. (2002). Preliminary evidence of efficacy for EMDR resource development and installation in the stabilization phase of treatment of complex posttraumatic stress disorder. *Journal of Clinical Psychology, 58,* 1465–1487.

Kornfield, J. (Ed.). (2010). *The Buddha is still teaching: Contemporary Buddhist wisdom.* Boston, MA: Shambhala Publications.

Shapiro, F. (1995). *Eye movement desensitization and reprocessing: Basic principles, protocols and procedures.* New York, NY: Guilford Press.

Shapiro, F. (2001). *Eye movement desensitization and reprocessing: Basic principles, protocols, and procedures* (2nd ed.). New York, NY: Guilford Press.

Van der Kolk, B. (2014). *The body keeps the score: Brain, mind, and body in the healing of trauma*. New York, NY: Viking.

World Health Organization. (2013). *Assessment and management of conditions specifically related to stress: mhGAP Intervention Guide Module*. Geneva, Switzerland: Author. Retrieved from http://apps.who.int/iris/bitstream/10665/85623/1/9789241505932_eng .pdf?ua=1

3

Developing Buddhist Mindfulness Practice for Trauma-Focused Care

NO CORRECT PATH TO MINDFULNESS PRACTICE

There is no such thing as a singular, correct path to a mindfulness practice. The experience of mindfulness presents itself in a variety of packages. One does not have to move to a monastery to begin working with Buddhist mindfulness or become a Buddhist to experience the practices and incorporate them into daily living. Indeed, many clients have first encountered the practice of mindfulness and begun to experience the benefits of this healing system in the context of a therapeutic setting. You, as the clinician, have the potential to be the first—and maybe the only—mindfulness teacher your clients will encounter on their path.

In this chapter, some specific coaching is given on starting a mindfulness practice for yourself so that you will be in a better position to share it with your clients. There is now a wealth of teachers, books, podcasts, retreat opportunities, meditation communities, and other resources for lay people to begin a practice. The instructions that many give today are variations or modern translations of practices introduced almost 2,600 years ago. Some of the core, foundational practices brought to us by the Buddha and some of his adherents over the millennia are spelled out in the next several pages. Even if you are an experienced mindfulness practitioner, you are encouraged to embrace the teaching and shaping of a beginner's mind as you work through this chapter. Working with the material in this way will allow you to better remember what it was like when you first set out on a mindful path, and can help you more fully empathize with clients who may be struggling with the practices.

STARTING A MINDFULNESS PRACTICE

Mindfulness practice will provide resources for our clients and help them deepen their trauma-reprocessing experience when they arrive at that point in their treatment. In addition to implementing resources to assist them in reprocessing traumatic memories, clients can discover that the mindful skills utilized in their treatment can be accessed continuously as they seek to live a more adaptive life. These practices will also help eye movement desensitization and reprocessing (EMDR) therapists as they attune to their clients, providing a safe and mindful container for the experience.

Moreover, these practices can help EMDR therapists to maintain a stable and resourced life of their own. Operating from this place of balance and self-care is vital for EMDR therapists, as we are likely to encounter high volumes of trauma and suffering daily. As *Against the Stream* Buddhist teacher Dave Smith (2016) observed in a Dharma talk, if you work in a paint store, it is very likely that you will end up with paint on yourself; there must be a plan in place, therefore, to clean yourself up. Similarly, if you work in the arena of human suffering, it is very likely that some of that suffering will cling to you. What is the plan you have in place to manage this reality and to clear away what may linger?

These practices do not have to be executed sequentially. Many Buddhist teachers recommend staying with both breath- and body-focused meditations first. This focus can help clients to develop that anchor of the present moment, utilize that resource, and take a break from their thoughts, at least for a while. Some clients, however, will need additional grounding, sights, or sounds, or specific body sensations before they can go to breath. At the end of each practice, some notes on modifications and special considerations are given; these may be especially useful for clients with more complex presentations who require further grounding. If a client seems to struggle with these more classical practices, please recognize that the skills presented here are not your only options for sharing mindfulness practice. There are more strategies of the creative/expressive variety covered in Chapters 4 and 6; further ideas are given for using these practices with clients who may resist them at every turn.

The scripts that follow in this chapter are designed for the use of the therapist and are presented in language that may serve as a guide in clinical settings. To reemphasize a major idea in this book: Make it personal. You will be in the best position to share these skills with your clients if you have first tried them on your own and experimented with how they can be used in your own life. It is important that clients learn the skills in the presence of the therapist so that both therapist and client feel that there is an understanding of how to use the meditation technique. The scripts in this chapter can be utilized so that clients may feel confident in their practice, and you are free to modify them to better reflect an individual client's developmental and educational needs. A worksheet in Chapter 9 can be used by clients to track the practices that work best for them in certain situations; an additional copy appears for your reference in the appendix.

Mindfulness of Breath/Sensory Grounding

There are a number of reasons why the Buddha suggested we use the breath as an object of meditation. It represents mindfulness of the body and it is our best body-oriented marker of moment-to-moment experience. Here, we combine it with grounding:

- Find a comfortable position. If sitting on a cushion, hold your spine as erect as possible. If sitting in a chair, try to support your own back; if you need support, please use it. Have your feet on the floor and rest your hands comfortably in your lap. The position should be sustainable for the length of your sitting.

- Settle into your posture. Scan around the points of contact: your back on the chair if you have chosen that option, your seat, the backs of your legs, feet on the floor, where the hands and arms meet the body. See if any of these points feel more grounded than the others. If you are not feeling particularly grounded at this moment, see if you can just notice that lack of grounded feeling, with as little judgment as possible.

- If you do experience your grounding to be stronger at one or more contact points, go ahead and lean into that grounding. Let yourself have that ground.

- After a minute or so, turn your attention toward your breath. Find the spot either just outside or just inside the nostrils, or notice the rise and fall of the belly. Any one of these is a great place to note the sensation of the breath going in and out. Which one you choose is not important, though it is wise to choose one for the length of this sitting.

- If it is helpful, you can add the anchor provided by one of the Buddha's simplest instructions: "When I am breathing in, I know I am breathing in; when I am breathing out, I know I am breathing out."

- It is the nature of the mind to think. When—not if—your mind begins to wander, just notice that it is happening. Gently note that you have wandered off the breath, with as little judgment as possible at that moment, and then return to noting the physical sensation of the breath.

- Set a timer, and continue this practice for a set period that feels appropriate and sustainable for your current level of practice. Five minutes a day is a good start for many. Five minutes a day is better than 30 minutes on Saturday. One minute is better than zero minutes. The development of a consistent practice is key.

FURTHER MODIFICATIONS FOR TRAUMA-FOCUSED CARE

○ Some clients may want to lie down. This adjustment can work, while it is helpful to gently let the client know the benefits of sitting up to maintain a sense of energy and awareness in addition to any relaxation that may occur.

○ If, in focusing on contact points, there is resistance or an inability to ground effectively, you can have clients open their eyes—if they are not open already—and scan the room and do grounding through sights in the room, objects, sounds, and so forth.

○ Some clients will not be able to feel the ground at all. Remind them of the instruction to notice the lack of ground. The work then becomes reducing judgment in a titrated fashion.

○ If the Buddha's instruction does not feel right as a verbal anchor, other mantra-like devices can be helpful—for example, "Breathing in, I am strong; breathing out, I release fear." Allow clients to choose their own.

○ The most important ongoing instruction is letting clients know that they will be thinking all the time, and that this is not a sign of failure. Mindfulness is not about turning the mind off; this is a common mistake. People who practice for decades will still have a thought about who is leading the National League in Major League Baseball, or finding recipes for tonight's dinner. Remind the client this is very, very, very normal.

○ If five minutes is not sustainable, offer clients the opportunity to decide how long they can sit. And then sit with them for that length of time, and provide the context of success that comes with that. As Hakuin, a 17th-century Zen master, said in his poem "Song of Zazen": "Even those who have practiced for just one sitting will be blessed most infinitely" (Suzuki, 1994; p. 151).

This foundational practice can be a primary practice for many clients, of course remembering that one size does not fit all. It represents one of the fundamental teachings of the Buddha regarding mindfulness. Just this practice can provide a lifetime of concentration and insight, although if you are attracted to it, you will most probably find yourself exploring some of the other practices of wisdom, ethics, and insight. For now, know that you may make this simple practice central to your experience of mindfulness.

Mindfulness of Feeling Tone

The second foundation of mindfulness described by the Buddha was Mindfulness of Feeling Tone. Often mistranslated as mindfulness of feeling, this gives the impression that we are tracking our emotions. In fact, the Buddha suggested that all sensations, emotions, and thoughts could be tracked to fall within one of three categories: pleasant, unpleasant, or neutral. This meditation allows us to begin that process of simplifying our relationship to our mind's constant opinions about our experience.

- Find a comfortable position. If sitting on a cushion, hold your spine as erect as possible. If sitting in a chair, try to support your own back; if you need support, please use it. Have your feet on the floor and rest your hands comfortably in your lap. The position should be sustainable for the length of your sitting.

- Settle into your posture. Scan around the points of contact: your back on the chair if you have chosen that option, your seat, the backs of your legs, feet on the floor, where the hands and arms meet the body. See if any of these points feel more grounded than the others. If you are not feeling particularly grounded at this moment, see if you can just notice that lack of grounded feeling with as little judgment as possible.

- If you do feel your grounding to be stronger at one or more contact points, go ahead and lean into that grounding. Let yourself have that ground.

- After a minute or so, turn your attention toward your breath. Find the spot either just outside or just inside the nostrils, or notice the rise and fall of the belly. Any one of these is a great place to note the sensation of the breath going in and out. Which one you choose is not important, though it is wise to choose one for the length of this sitting.

- Begin to more carefully track general body sensations, thoughts, and feelings. If you notice a physical sensation, rate it on the scale of pleasant, unpleasant, or neutral. As you continue to track physical sensations, you might wander toward feelings, thoughts, sounds, and other sensory stimuli. Have a goal of beginning to find the rhythm of pleasant, unpleasant, or neutral being the only thought you are having in each moment.

- It is the nature of the mind to think. When—not if—your mind begins to wander, just notice that it is happening. In this meditation, we can notice if this wandering is, in fact, pleasant, unpleasant, or neutral. Then, continue to find your way back to the rating system as you resume tracking your experience.

- Set a timer and continue this practice for a length of time that feels appropriate and sustainable for your current level of practice. Five minutes a day is a good start for many. Five minutes a day is better than 30 minutes on Saturday. One minute is better than zero minutes. The development of a consistent practice is key.

FURTHER MODIFICATIONS FOR TRAUMA-FOCUSED CARE

○ Some clients may want to lie down. This adjustment can work, while it is helpful to gently let the client know the benefits of sitting up to maintain a sense of energy and awareness in addition to any relaxation that may occur.

○ Some clients will not be able to feel the ground at all. Remind them of the instruction to notice the lack of ground. This particular meditation may help in reducing judgment, as it levels the playing field regarding our experiences.

○ Some clients may feel the need to change the verbiage to make it their own. Encourage them to do so, while in the spirit of finding words for these three categories of pleasant, unpleasant, or neutral.

○ The most important ongoing instruction is letting clients know that they will be thinking all the time, and that this is not a sign of failure. In this meditation, categories are used to give structure to our internal experience. We are not turning the mind off; this is a common mistake in the teaching of mindfulness. People who practice for decades will still have a thought about where they left their favorite T-shirt five years ago or solving some problem from the work day. Remind the client this is very, very, very normal. In this case, the instruction is to simply notice if the thought about the T-shirt is pleasant, unpleasant, or neutral.

○ If five minutes is not sustainable, offer clients the opportunity to decide how long they can sit. And then sit with them for that length of time, and provide the context of success that comes with that. As modern-day mindfulness teachers such as Sharon Salzberg and Jon Kabat-Zinn often remind us: *If you can breathe, you can meditate.*

This practice of feeling tone represents one of the primary teachings of the Buddha regarding mindfulness. This practice helps us to have the direct experience that the Buddha had—that we tend to crave and cling to pleasant experiences and be averse to and run away from painful experiences. Neutral experience tends to make us dull and shift into a state of mindlessness. Here, we are focusing on these states to establish a greater mindfulness of how our mind actually works and to start to neutralize the effects of craving, clinging, and aversion.

Mindfulness of Mind

The third foundation of mindfulness described by the Buddha was Mindfulness of Mind or Mindfulness of Thinking. The word for mind, *citta*, more accurately translates as "heart/mind." Thus, our attention goes toward emotional states related to consciousness as well. There are many meditations associated with this category, including labeling, noticing the passing of thoughts as clouds or a river, or simply awareness of the variety of states of consciousness as they arrive and pass. As with the other foundations, the most important aspect is the lack or attempted decreasing of judgment, moving toward dispassionate observation of impersonal states of mind and heart.

- Find a comfortable position. If sitting on a cushion, hold your spine as erect as possible. If sitting in a chair, try to support your own back; if you need support, please use it. Have your feet on the floor and rest your hands comfortably in your lap. The position should be sustainable for the length of your sitting.

- Settle into your posture. Scan around the points of contact: your back on the chair if you have chosen that option, your seat, the backs of your legs, feet on the floor, where the hands and arms meet the body. See if any of these points feel more grounded than the others. If you are not feeling particularly grounded at this moment, see if you can just notice that lack of grounded feeling with as little judgment as possible.

- If you experience your grounding to be stronger at one or more contact points, go ahead and lean into that grounding. Let yourself have that ground.

- After a minute or so, turn your attention toward your breath. Find the spot either just outside or just inside the nostrils, or notice the rise and fall of the belly. Any one of these is a great place to note the sensation of the breath going in and out. Which one you choose is not important, though it is wise to choose one for the length of this sitting.

- Begin to more carefully track thoughts and emotions, as well as states of consciousness related to body sensations such as being tired or alert. Begin to find a rhythm in noticing the arrival of these states of mind. As you do, you will also possibly notice when these states pass; this provides space to notice the arrival of another state. Notice your level of judgment of each state as simply another thought form.

- It is the nature of the mind to think. When—not if—your mind begins to wander, just notice that it is happening. You can label it along the lines of, "I am now in wandering mind . . . ." In this meditation, we can notice if this wandering continues or abates. Then, continue to notice the arising and passing states of mind.

- Set a timer, and continue this practice for a time period that feels appropriate and sustainable for your current level of practice. Five minutes a day to start with is generally recommended. Five minutes a day is better than 30 minutes on Saturday. One minute is better than zero minutes. The development of a practice is key. You may find that this particular practice requires a longer sitting, and it therefore may be something you come to later in your practice.

FURTHER MODIFICATIONS FOR TRAUMA-FOCUSED CARE

- Some clients may want to lie down. This adjustment can work, while it is helpful to gently let the client know over time the benefits of sitting up in order to maintain a sense of energy and awareness in addition to any relaxation that may occur.

- Some clients will not be able to feel the ground at all. Remind them of the instruction to notice the lack of ground. This particular meditation may help in reducing judgment, as it levels the playing field regarding our experiences.

- Some clients may feel the need to change the verbiage to make it their own. Encourage them to do so, while in the spirit of finding words for the nonjudgmental awareness of the various heart/mind states.

- The most important ongoing instruction is letting clients know that they will be thinking all the time, and that this is not a sign of failure. We are not turning the mind off; this is a common mistake in the teaching of mindfulness. People who practice for decades will still have a thought about who was the 14th president of the United States or realizing that the car needs an oil change. In this meditation, we can simply notice, "I am thinking about presidents and my car." Remind the client this is very, very, very normal. In this case, we are simply noticing that our mind is landing on presidents and cars. There is no judgment of the topic—simply noticing.

○ If five minutes is not sustainable, offer clients the opportunity to decide how long they can sit. And then sit with them for that length of time, and provide the context of success that comes with that. As Noah Levine (2007) has taught, "Just get to the cushion and notice what is there" (p. 132).

This practice represents one of the primary teachings of the Buddha regarding mindfulness. This practice may be more difficult for clients in early recovery, and may make more sense after some time with Mindfulness of Breath/Body and Mindfulness of Feeling Tone. This practice helps us to have the direct experience that the Buddha had, which was that humans tend to have a "monkey mind" that wanders from thought to thought. In this retraining of the brain, we can notice individual states of consciousness without mindlessly heading to the next thought that comes from the original thought or feeling. Here, we are focusing on these states to establish a greater mindfulness of how our mind really works, and to start neutralizing the effects of craving, clinging, and aversion. We teach clients how to develop a more robust mindfulness of moment-to-moment experience.

Mindfulness of Dharmas/Loving Kindness Meditation

The Fourth Foundation of Mindfulness described by the Buddha was Mindfulness of Dharmas, or Mindfulness of Greater Truths. This is where the meditator ponders some or all of the core teachings of the Buddha. These can include the Five Hindrances (Sensory Pleasure, Ill Will, Sloth and Torpor, Restlessness, and Doubt); the Three Poisons of Greed, Anger, and Delusion; the Three Marks of Existence of Impermanence, Suffering, and Not-Self; and any number of other matters of conceptual thought that will allow the meditator to gain a deeper understanding. One of the preferred groupings of meditations along these lines are the Four Divine Abodes, or the *Brahmaviharas*: loving kindness, compassion, appreciative joy, and equanimity. These are the fruits of Buddhist mindfulness practice, but they can also be cultivated on their own.

Loving Kindness meditation has become one of the most used meditative practices of the 21st century, thanks to the work of Sharon Salzberg (who brought the practice to the United States from Burma) and other teachers in the Insight Tradition of meditation, including Joseph Goldstein, Jack Kornfield, and Noah Levine. What follows is a version of Loving Kindness meditation based on the work of all these teachers:

- Find a comfortable position. If sitting on a cushion, hold your spine as erect as possible. If sitting in a chair, try to support your own back; if you need support, please use it. Have your feet on the floor and rest your hands comfortably in your lap. The position should be sustainable for the length of your sitting.

- Settle into your posture. Scan the points of contact: your back on the chair if you have chosen that option, your seat, the backs of your legs, feet on the floor, where the hands and arms meet the body. See if any of these points feel more grounded than the others. If you are not feeling particularly grounded at this moment, see if you can just notice that lack of grounded feeling with as little judgment as possible.

- If you do feel your grounding to be stronger at one or more contact points, go ahead and lean into that grounding. Let yourself have that ground.

- After a minute or so, turn your attention toward your breath. Find the spot either just outside or just inside the nostrils, or notice the rising and falling of the belly. Any one of these is a great place to note the sensation of the breath going in and out. Which one you choose is not important, though it is wise to choose one for the length of this sitting.

- Begin to silently say the Loving Kindness phrases, first toward yourself: "May I be free from fear, may I be healthy, may I be happy, may I be at ease." Send the phrases to yourself a few times. Then move on to someone to whom it is extremely easy for you to send the phrases, someone to whom unconditional love flows in one direction or both. Then, send it to a neutral person, someone for whom you have no particular positive or negative feeling. Then, send loving kindness to a difficult person—not necessarily the worst person in the world, just someone to whom you find it difficult to send those phrases. Then radiate it out in all directions, proceeding as slowly or as quickly as you wish: to everyone on my block . . . my city . . . my state . . . my country . . . my hemisphere . . . the world . . . all sentient beings in the world . . . all sentient beings in all known and unknown universes. Finally, land with one last round of loving kindness toward ourselves.

- It is the nature of the mind to think. When—not if—your mind begins to wander, just notice that it is happening. Then return to the phrases, noticing any discomfort or resistance. These become part of our process.

- Set a timer and continue this practice for a time period that feels appropriate and sustainable for your current level of practice. Five minutes a day is a good start for many. Five minutes a day is better than 30 minutes on Saturday. One minute is better than zero minutes. The development of a practice is key. You may find that this particular practice requires a longer sitting, and therefore may be something you come to later in your practice.

FURTHER MODIFICATIONS FOR TRAUMA-FOCUSED CARE

○ Some clients may want to lie down. This adjustment can work, while it is helpful to gently let the client know over time the benefits of sitting up in order to maintain a sense of energy and awareness in addition to any relaxation that may occur.

○ Some clients will not be able to feel the ground at all. Remind them of the instruction to notice the lack of ground. This particular meditation may help in reducing judgment, as it levels the playing field regarding our experiences.

○ Some clients may feel the need to change the verbiage to make it their own. Encourage them to do so, while in the spirit of finding words for the nonjudgmental awareness of the various aspects of loving kindness. Also, some clients may need to spend some time sending the loving kindness only in one direction, perhaps for a benefactor who has helped their recovery or for someone who they know loves them unconditionally or for whom they have those feelings. Some clients may initially find it difficult to send loving kindness to themselves or to people they find difficult.

○ The most important ongoing instruction is to let clients know that they will be thinking all the time, and that this is not a sign of failure. We are not turning the mind off; this is a common mistake in the teaching of mindfulness. People who practice for decades will still have a thought about the third season of *The Simpsons* or undone items on their to-do list that interrupts their focus on the phrases. In this meditation, we can simply notice, "I am thinking about Homer"; "I am thinking about stuff I have to do." Remind the client this is very, very, very normal. In this case, we are simply noticing that our mind is landing on baseball and apple pie, and then returning to the phrases. There is no judgment of the straying—simply noticing.

○ If five minutes is not sustainable, offer clients the opportunity to decide how long they can sit. And then sit with them for that length of time, and provide the context of success that comes with that despite any difficulties they have. As Joseph Goldstein (1993) said in his book *Insight Meditation*, "Our progress in meditation does not depend on the measure of pleasure or pain in our experience. Rather, the quality of our practice has to do with how open we are to whatever is there" (p. 47). Our clients can become more open to their experience in very small increments, if necessary.

This practice of loving kindness represents one of the primary teachings of the Buddha regarding mindfulness. It helps us to have the direct experience that the Buddha had, which was that when we focus on these dharmas, we tend to find ourselves cultivating the very states upon which we are concentrating. Other practices help these states to arise, but we can bring them about right here, right now. Here, clients can focus on these states in order to establish a greater sense of the role of loving kindness, and to start to neutralize the effects of craving, clinging, and aversion. Clinicians can assist clients in developing a more robust mindfulness of moment-to-moment experience, and the possibility of cultivating loving kindness, compassion, appreciative joy, and equanimity throughout these moments.

Walking Meditation

Walking meditation has a millennia-old tradition in Buddhist practice. In many ways, one could consider it part of the bridge from classical mindfulness practice to the more modern innovations, often drawn from a variety of millennia-old practices from other cultures, of creating more formal practice using movement-based pathways. The Buddha discussed experiencing mindfulness in what he called all four postures—sitting, standing, walking, and lying down. Lying down remains our go-to posture for those who can meditate in no other manner. Walking meditation takes the client off the cushion or off the floor, and adds the simplest motion to the act of mindfulness.

- Find a comfortable standing position. Map out a pathway in front of you, a distance of six to eight feet with no obstructions. You will simply be walking back and forth in this path.

- Begin your stride: in super-slow motion, a regular gait, or something in between. We tend to prefer in between, perhaps mimicking the bilateral stimulation speed we use for resourcing in EMDR therapy.

- You may simply notice your walking, or you can use anchoring phrases such as lifting, moving, placing, or shifting. Either way, keep your gaze at a 45-degree angle. The goal is not to look around, which might promote the wandering mind. We are focused on the act of walking, perhaps our breathing, and the accompanying body sensations.

- After a minute or so, turn your attention toward your breath. Find the spot either just outside or just inside the nostrils, or notice the rise and fall of the belly. Any one of these is a great place to note the sensation of the breath going in and out. Which one you choose is not important, though it is wise to choose one for this walking meditation.

- Continue to walk back and forth on this path for the time you allot for the meditation.

- It is the nature of the mind to think. When—not if—your mind begins to wander, just notice that it is happening. Then return to your body and its practice of walking.

- Set a timer and continue this practice for a time period that feels appropriate and sustainable for your current level of practice. Five minutes a day is a good start for many. Five minutes a day is better than 30 minutes on Saturday. One minute is better than zero minutes. The development of a practice is key.

FURTHER MODIFICATIONS FOR TRAUMA-FOCUSED CARE

- Some clients will not be able to feel they are grounded at all during walking meditation. Remind them of the instruction to notice the lack of ground. This particular meditation may help in reducing judgment, as it puts the practitioner a little more squarely in their body-oriented experience of movement.

- Some clients may feel the need to change the verbiage of an anchoring phrase to make it their own. Encourage them to do so, while in the spirit of finding words for the nonjudgmental awareness of the various aspects of walking.

- The most important ongoing instruction is to let clients know that they will be thinking all the time, and that this is not a sign of failure. This practice, like others, is not about turning the mind off. This is a common mistake in the teaching of mindfulness. People who practice for decades will still have a thought about what their third-grade teacher is up to now or how many dominoes make up a set. In this meditation, we can simply notice "I am thinking about third-grade teachers" or "I am thinking about dominoes," and return to our walking. Remind the client this is very, very, very normal. In this case, we are simply noticing that our mind is landing on third grade or dominoes, and then returning to our focus on our walking—simply noticing.

○ If five minutes is not sustainable in walking practice, clinicians offer clients the opportunity to decide how long they can walk. Then walk with them for that length of time and provide the context of success that comes with that. The reference to Hakuin's poem "Song of Zazen" still applies: "Even those who have practiced for just one sitting will be blessed most infinitely." Walking practice has similar power.

Walking meditation represents one of the primary teachings of the Buddha regarding mindfulness. This practice helps individuals to have the direct experience that the Buddha had, which was that human beings can practice in any posture, not just sitting. Practitioners from all walks of life start to neutralize the effects of craving, clinging, and aversion. Clinicians teaching this meditation to clients are facilitating a more robust mindfulness of moment-to-moment experience, and the possibility to cultivate meaningful practice throughout the day in all the activities of our lives.

Beginner's Mind Practice

Some practitioners in the Zen Buddhist tradition wrestle with a spiritual training tool called a *koan*, which presents one with a problem that cannot be solved with the rational mind. Others practice *shikantaza*, which literally means "just sitting." For the beginner, it is generally best to include an anchor, and many Zen teachers add the simple anchoring practice of counting the breaths. This practice is a helpful addition to any mindfulness practice because it is portable. Practitioners can do it anywhere, anytime.

● Find a comfortable position. If sitting on a cushion, hold your spine as erect as possible. If sitting in a chair, try to support your own back; if you need support, please use it. Have your feet on the floor and rest your hands comfortably in your lap. The position should be sustainable for the length of your sitting.

● Settle into your posture. Scan around the points of contact: your back on the chair if you have chosen that option, your seat, the backs of your legs, feet on the floor, where the hands and arms meet the body. See if any of these points feel more grounded than the others. If you are not feeling particularly grounded at this moment, see if you can just notice that lack of grounded feeling with as little judgment as possible.

● If you experience your grounding to be stronger at one or more contact points, go ahead and lean into that grounding. Let yourself have that ground.

- After a minute or so, turn your attention toward your breath. Find the spot either just outside or just inside the nostrils, or notice the rise and fall of the belly. Any one of these is a great place to note the sensation of the breath going in and out. Which one you choose is not important, though it is wise to choose one for the length of this sitting.

- As you continue to notice your breathing, breathe into silence. On the out breath, count out *one*. Follow with a silent in breath, then, silently count *two* on the out breath. When you notice your mind wandering (which it will), simply start your count again at *one*. Anytime you make it to *10*, simply restart your count at *one*. This is the whole practice!

- It is the nature of the mind to think. When—not if—your mind begins to wander, just notice that it is happening. Gently note that you have wandered off the breath, with as little judgment as possible at that moment, and return to noting the physical sensation of the breath.

- Set a timer and continue this practice for a time period that feels appropriate and sustainable for your current level of practice. As in all our meditations, five minutes a day to start with is recommended. Five minutes a day is better than 30 minutes on Saturday. One minute is better than zero minutes. The development of a practice is key.

FURTHER MODIFICATIONS FOR TRAUMA-FOCUSED CARE

- If the client chooses to lie down, this is an option. Going forward, however, it is helpful to remind the client that a seated position helps in maintaining awareness along with the relaxation that may eventually help in moving on to the postures.

- Clients who have a hard time with breath and body as an anchor may scan the room for objects, naming them as they see them. This can be the entire meditation, or it can be a way to move on to the breath and body.

- Some clients will not be able to feel the ground at all. Remind them of the instruction to notice the lack of ground. The work then becomes on reducing judgment in a titrated fashion.

- If counting does not resonate with the client, see if there is another tracking method that will work for them. One alternative would be silently thinking *in* on the in breath and *out* on the out breath. One could also note the physical sensation of the breath as it touches the nostrils, or the rise and the fall of the belly. Allow clients to choose their own.

○ The most important ongoing instruction is to let clients know that they will be thinking all the time, and that thinking is not a sign of failure. We are not asking clients to turn the mind off. This is a common mistake in the teaching of mindfulness. People who practice for decades will still have a thought about the difference between pine trees and oak trees, or finding a good bagel store nearby. Remind the client this is very, very, very normal.

○ If five minutes is not sustainable, offer clients the opportunity to decide how long they can sit. And then sit with them for that length of time, and provide the context of success that comes with that. As Hakuin, the 17th-century Zen master, said in his poem "Song of Zazen": "Even those who have practiced for just one sitting will be blessed most infinitely."

This *beginner's mind* practice represents one of the primary teachings of the Buddha regarding mindfulness. Just this practice can provide a lifetime of concentration and insight, although if you are attracted to it you will probably find yourself exploring the other practices of wisdom, ethics, and insight. For now, know that you may make this simple practice central to your experience of mindfulness. For the clinician and the client, developing this muscle of returning to beginner's mind, again and again, produces the benefits of ongoing presence in the therapy room, deeper attunement to self and other, and the spirit of curiosity that helps the process of "just notice" and "go with that" to move forward.

TYING IT ALL TOGETHER

Buddhist Mindfulness has been a powerful psychological and spiritual tool for over two and a half millennia. Modern science has backed up its efficacy for a number of disorders and difficulties. The Buddha's inclination and instruction to go toward and even into the suffering is something that psychologists of more than one theoretical orientation have for decades described as an intervention.

The mindfulness instructions provided here reflect the original wisdom of the Buddha's Four Noble Truths and his Eightfold Path. The Buddha noted that life contains suffering; that suffering is caused by craving, clinging, and aversion; and that suffering can end by treating these difficulties. Through mindfulness skills, clinicians and other helping professionals are empowering clients to discover these truths for themselves. Self-discovery can facilitate a meaningful healing process in a manner similar to what happens when clients make their own connections in EMDR therapy. When combined with EMDR therapy, mindfulness empowers them to participate much more powerfully in their own resourcing and reprocessing experiences.

This empowerment is at the heart of all that we do as EMDR therapists. This gift of mindfulness, then, can remain for a lifetime, long after our time with the client has ended.

QUESTIONS FOR REFLECTION AND PERSONAL PRACTICE

- What was my personal experience with engaging in the practices described in this chapter?

- Do any of the practices in this chapter resonate with me more than others? What does this identified resonance teach me about myself and my journey thus far?

- Do I resist any of the practices in this chapter, or find any of them uncomfortable? What lessons are there to be learned from this resistance or discomfort?

- How can I implement one or more of these practices into my daily life?

RESOURCES FOR FURTHER EXPLORATION

Chodron, P. (2013). *How to meditate: A practical guide to making friends with your mind.* Boulder, CO: Sounds True.

Dansiger, S. (2016). *Clinical dharma: A path for healers and helpers.* Los Angeles, CA: StartAgain Media.

Kabat-Zinn, J. (1994). *Wherever you go, there you are: Mindfulness meditation in everyday life.* New York, NY: Hyperion.

Kornfield, J. (2008). *Meditation for beginners.* Boulder, CO: Sounds True.

Salzberg, S. (1995). *Lovingkindness: The revolutionary art of happiness.* Boston, MA: Shambhala.

REFERENCES

Goldstein, J. (1993). *Insight meditation: The practice of freedom.* Boston, MA: Shambhala Publications.

Levine, N. (2007). *Against the stream: A Buddhist manual for spiritual revolutionaries.* New York, NY: HarperCollins.

Smith, D. (2016, April 9). *Clinical dharma & self-care.* Presented at the Clinical Dharma Half Day Retreat, Against the Stream Santa Monica, Santa Monica, CA.

Suzuki, D.T. (1994). *Manual of Zen Buddhism.* New York: Grove/Atlantic.

4

An Introduction to the Creative Mindfulness Practices

Many of the classic mindfulness practices described in the previous chapter are traditionally done in the context of a seated or still posture. Can the essence of the Buddha's teachings and the benefits of mindfulness meditation be experienced in activities other than sitting still? Can one truly cultivate mindfulness while engaging in activities that can be described as more expressive or creative? Can one, perhaps, enter mindful practice while dancing to music by Lady Gaga or The Ramones?

Of course.

Consider that in 2008, the great Buddhist monk Thich Nhat Hahn wrote a beautiful volume called *Mindful Movements* that featured his 10 favorite stretches to do in between seated meditation practices. Even the classic practice of walking meditation, developed in Buddhist monastic tradition and covered in the previous chapter, demonstrates the need for adaptation and flexibility in practice. This chapter further explores some of these creative modifications and discusses their relevance for modern clients in need of trauma-informed services.

Trauma-focused eye movement desensitization and reprocessing (EMDR) therapy requires clinicians to broaden their skill sets for the delivery of Phase 2, Preparation. Learning one Calm Safe Place exercise is generally not sufficient. A major theme of this book is that teaching the core skills of mindfulness can enhance what you are able to do in Phase 2 as an EMDR therapist. This enhancement does not apply just to stabilization components. Rather, the teaching and cultivation of mindfulness skills in Phase 2 offers clients critical orientation in what it means to notice something in the body, or to simply be present to experience without judging it. Many EMDR therapists, armed for Phase 2 with only the Calm Safe Place and Light Stream guided visualizations from basic, can be met with blank stares from clients when they move in later phases of the protocol. It is common to hear such questions as "What do you mean, *what am I noticing in my body*?" or "What are you talking about, *go with that* or *what are you getting now*?" Such questions can disrupt the flow of the reprocessing work after a person is already activated. Orienting clients to the essence of these prompting questions used in EMDR therapy is best accomplished through mindfulness-informed orientation in Phase 2.

You received a crash course in how to begin offering this orientation in Chapter 3. This chapter offers even more creative ways to teach mindfulness and share the spirit of what it means to be mindful. The specific practices are muscle clenching and releasing, transforming day-to-day activities into meditation, movement practices, yogic breathing practices, and approaching the expressive arts (e.g., drawing, music making/listening, dance) with meditative intention. It may be tempting to skim through some of these exercises and see them suited best for children, because they are more creative and movement-based. Please refrain from making that assumption. Some of the most fulfilling experiences teaching these exercises can happen with adults who are hungry for a fresh, active, and expressive way to learn.

YOGIC BREATHING PRACTICES

Before progressing into this series of breath practices, it is generally advisable to begin with some of the basic, classic breath awareness practices described in the previous chapter. If a client can tolerate the general experience of tracking breath, you may consider moving to one or many breath practices often taught in yoga. As with all of the practices, it is important to have a solid sense of how to use these breath practices yourself before showing them to clients. If you need extra assistance with learning these practices, consider taking a couple of yoga classes in your community or visit the resources offered at the end of this chapter to locate some complimentary online videos of guided breath meditations.

A few general notes about breath before moving into the specific practices: Not every client will like each of these breath practices. In teaching them, it is generally important to offer them as options and then let your clients decide which breath practices will best serve them and when. Do not present any sophisticated counting patterns or skills involving holds and counts, such as Box Breathing or 4-4-4-4 breath. Although these exercises are not necessarily contraindicated if a client can tolerate them, introducing too much holding of the breath with traumatized clients who are new to breath work can induce panic and a sense of dread. Although you can add holds and sophisticated count patterns later in the instruction or as modifications, they are generally not required to begin breath practice.

A trauma-informed safety note on these breath practices: Eyes do not have to be closed. You can also go very slowly. For clients who struggle with dissociation or getting relaxed, one full breath can be a major initial achievement. Consider having clients with a tendency to dissociate hold onto a hard-textured element, such as a rock, marble, or stone, for further grounding as they experiment with the various breath practices.

Diaphragmatic Breathing (Belly Breathing)

Have you ever watched an infant breathe? If so, you will notice that babies naturally breathe with their bellies. Somewhere along the way, we seem to lose this natural tendency and develop rapid, shallow breathing that originates in the chest. Like all elements of mindful breathing, belly breathing takes practice. If you or your clients have a tendency to self-criticize for not *doing it right*, simply invite the breath pattern back to what seems like any natural beginning place. As the Roman Catholic mystic St. Benedict taught (congruous with the Buddhist idea of beginner's mind): *Always we can begin again.* Here are some basic steps to begin the practice:

- Put one or both hands on the upper area of your stomach so that you can pay attention to the movement of your diaphragm.

- As you inhale through your nose, allow your belly to expand as far as it will go.

- Exhale through your mouth, allowing the belly to pull back in.

- Continue this inhale–exhale pattern at your own pace, giving it at least six to seven repetitions (about one minute) to find a rhythm and style that work for you.

FURTHER MODIFICATIONS AND OPTIONS FOR CREATIVITY

○ Start small. If the suggested numbers of repetitions or lengths seem too overwhelming, you can begin with just one full breath, reevaluate, and then decide if you wish to continue with more consecutive repetitions.

○ If clients feel awkward or in any way out of control with this suggested pattern, consider starting with an exhale instead of an inhale.

○ After initially experimenting with the breath and finding a rhythm, consider puckering the mouth slightly and lengthening the exhales. For some people, a longer exhale enhances the relaxation experience.

○ If paying attention to the breath on its own is not working for your clients, consider adding a count to it (e.g., *in "one," out "one"; in "two," out "two"*) and continuing to 10, then returning to resume the count at one). Adding this type of count for modification is not about holding the breath; rather, using the numbers as an anchor helps you stay focused on the task at hand—breathing. You can also add a word or a special phrase (e.g., *"Satnam*;" "amen," "help me," "as I breathe in, I know I am breathing in; as I breathe out, I know I am breathing out").

○ You can engage the young (or the young at heart) in this practice by having them put a Beanie Baby or a flat type of stuffed animal on the stomach to provide a focus point for observing the rise and fall of the belly.

Diaphragmatic breathing is a classic starting point in teaching breath, and many clinicians may have been taught how to do it in earlier training. It is an important foundation for teaching the other breath practices in this chapter. Even though variations and creative twists will be presented, the general rule is to originate all the breath practices that follow with the deep inhale as the belly expands.

Complete Breathing (Three-Part or Dirgha Breathing)

Think of a complete breath as a three-part breath, with the diaphragmatic part of the breath being the first step. The complete breath, as the name suggests, is a fuller breath, inviting us to engage the breath in two more places (i.e., the ribs and the lungs). Here are the steps:

● Begin with a diaphragmatic breath. Continue inhaling into the ribs, and then, the chest. You can put one hand on the stomach and one hand on the chest to help with maintaining your awareness.

● At the top of the inhale, notice the breath. If it causes you pain or distress to observe the breath like this, even for a moment, you can release right into the exhale.

● Gradually release the breath with your exhale, allowing the chest, the ribs, and the belly to pull back in.

---

*Sanskrit for "I am truth"

- Continue this inhale–exhale pattern at your own pace, giving it at least six to seven repetitions (about one minute) to find a rhythm and style that work for you.

Further Modifications and Options for Creativity

○ As with all of the exercises suggested in this book, you can vary how long you spend in each practice or how many repetitions you attempt based on your experience on a given day. As a clinician guiding these practices, it is important to work with feedback from the client in offering time guidelines.

○ The standard pattern with exhales is to keep them slow and deliberate. However, a very powerful variation is to do a fast, dramatic exhale, like a sigh of relief.

○ Feel free to get as dramatic as you want on the exhale, perhaps bringing the hand to the forehead and exhaling all of the drama! Master EMDR therapist and educator Amber Stiles-Bodnar calls this variation the "drama queen breath" with her teenage clients. Think of this breath as a chance to let go of negative energy and the things that no longer serve you.

○ When you expand your chest on the inhale, you can bring up "super-hero" imagery to further the empowering motion. To bring in the other expressive arts, maybe invite your clients to cue up a favorite song from a superhero movie and breathe along.

As a practice, some people resonate more with complete breathing because they like the experience of taking a deeper, fuller breath. While many clients may like the breath for that reason, just as many others can be intimidated and even scared by taking too deep a breath too early in their process. Knowledge of all these different breath practices and their variations is important so that you can respond to client feedback with different strategies and modifications of those strategies.

Ujjayi Breathing (Ocean-Sounding Victory Breath)

So many of the therapeutically beneficial breath practices taught in yoga and meditation settings invite an *in through the nose, out through the mouth* pattern. Ocean breath is fundamentally different: the general instruction is to breathe in through the nose and *out* through the nose. If you make a certain formation with your mouth and throat, you can mimic the sound of the ocean! Or you may like to think of it as the sound of the infamous Darth Vader. This breath is excellent for enduring stress, physical or mental:

- Pucker your mouth as if you are sucking through a straw or about to kiss someone. Try to contract the back of your throat so that it is slightly closed.

- Inhale through your nose; your belly should expand with this motion.

- Exhale through your nose; although air may flow out of your mouth, think about doing the work with your nose.

- If your mouth is puckered and your throat constricted, you should be producing the sound of the ocean.

- Attempt to keep the inhales and exhales even, especially while you are first learning the breath.

- If you are new to this breath, do not attempt more than five full repetitions during your first attempt. Starting slowly can be an important modification of all the breath practices that have therapeutic benefit, but it is especially important with this very dynamic breath.

- It is completely normal to feel somewhat lightheaded, but it should be a "good" lightheaded feeling. If it does not feel good, chances are you tried too many too soon, or the inhales and exhales were uneven.

FURTHER MODIFICATIONS AND OPTIONS FOR CREATIVITY

○ You can envision different characters with this breath, like Darth Vader or a charging bull that huffs and puffs. You may be surprised at what movie references or other creative anchors work for your clients.

○ Get a mirror and see the steam created by your breath on the surface (young people, especially, enjoy this). It creates an image of your breath as "the Force."

○ You and your clients can visualize, on any breath, that you are inhaling a calming or soothing color and exhaling a color that represents stress.

This breath is such a vital tool for trauma-focused clinicians. Because it so directly stimulates the vagus nerve, this breath can be very powerful in helping people move through fight, flight, or freeze responses. If done preventatively (e.g., before going into a situation that is known to be highly stressful), this breath can assist clients in staying calm and grounded during a stressful situation. The breath can also feel more relevant, dynamic, and applicable to clients who struggle with the relative gentleness of simple diaphragmatic breathing. Another tool for engaging clients with this breath can be to invite an inhale with an "angry face" expression, and experiment with releasing the anger or tension on the exhale.

Lion Breathing

Although taking on the full character of a lion is optional with this exercise, making the face of a lion with this breath can help with releasing negative energy and sensing inner confidence.

- Begin with a healthy inhale, from the belly.
- Exhale vigorously, allowing the tongue to hang out. Feel the jaw and cheeks loosen. Open the eyes widely to help with this release.
- Try at least five full repetitions, although you can continue with this breath as long as is physically comfortable. On the flip side, it is fine if one full breath is all you can manage at on your first attempt.

FURTHER MODIFICATIONS AND OPTIONS FOR CREATIVITY

- This is a wonderful exercise to teach children (or adults who are not too self-conscious to try it). You can think of making this face when ugly thoughts about trauma or stress come up.
- Consider how embodying the strength or character of a lion can help you breathe through a painful trigger with strength and confidence. Bringing in other expressive arts elements, such as costume making or acting out a scene, may help your client further develop the breath as a resource.

This breath is simply good fun! If you are working with clients in a group setting and the tone of the group has gotten very serious or tense, teaching this breath can be an excellent way to lighten the mood and promote laughter. In EMDR therapy, it can also have a tremendous benefit in reprocessing if a client is experiencing a sense of being stuck in the throat or another area of expression. Inviting a few rounds of lion breathing can be an excellent clearing device.

Alternate Nostril Breathing (Nadhi Shodnan Pranayama)

This is one of the best breath practices you can use to start teaching your clients about bilateral stimulation and how it can be used to balance the brain. The Sanskrit name for this breath, *nadhi shodnan pranayama*, is used by yogis and translates as "energy cleansing breath."

- Use your right thumb to plug off your right nostril at the side. Take a moment to notice this and make sure it is not too uncomfortable.

- Inhale with the left side of your nostril using a diaphragmatic or complete breath.

- Hold the breath for a moment, then use your right pinky to plug off the left nostril at the side.

- Exhale through the right nostril.

- Inhale again through the right nostril and repeat this alternating process as long as it is comfortable.

FURTHER MODIFICATIONS AND OPTIONS FOR CREATIVITY

- If you or a client is left-handed, the left hand can be used as the dominant hand for the exercise.

- Another useful hand position is to make "peace fingers" with the index and middle finger and place them in the center of the forehead; there is also a pressure point here that can help promote relaxation. From this position, you can easily manipulate the thumb to block off one nostril and the ring or pinky finger to block off the other.

- This breath may at first be too triggering for clients who dissociate or struggle with embodiment—as may any that promotes a conscious holding of the breath. If necessary, shorten the length of each set and the overall length of the exercise.

- A benefit of this breath is that it gives clients something to do with their hands as they are breathing. Many feel that this additional task requires an extra layer of required concentration, making it less likely for the mind to wander.

- Consider having clients access this breath before and after you work with one of the movement-based exercises covered in this chapter, and discover how the combination may serve you.

- It is very common for the sinuses to begin clearing with this breath: keeping tissues nearby is a good idea!

The practice is a solid way to orient clients to the healing power of dual attention stimulus, but many clients are likely to have a love–hate relationship with this breath. Some will notice the benefits right away; others will say they do not notice much of a benefit. This is a strategy that, more so than with some of the other breath practices, may require practice over time for the benefit to sink in.

CLENCH AND RELEASE: A MODIFIED PROGRESSIVE MUSCLE RELAXATION EXPERIENCE

Progressive muscle relaxation is a hypnotherapy technique from the 1920s with which many helping professionals are familiar. A full progressive muscle relaxation experience, in which individuals clench and release one muscle group at a time, can exceed 15 or 20 minutes. The ancient practice of *yoga nidra*, often called the yoga of divine rest, may also make use of similar clenching and release patterns to induce deep relaxation, depending on the lineage and tradition of the practice. This exercise developed out of the need clients verbalized for a more "express" version of the progressive muscle relaxation practice that they can access when they have only a few minutes to become more present to their body's experiences in a given moment and release some tension in the process. If working with dissociation or complex trauma, it is generally wise to teach this exercise before breathing or guided visualization exercises. Because this exercise works directly with body sensation, it serves as an excellent anchor should any of those other exercises prove problematic.

Here are the basic steps of this exercise:

- Make fists.

- You can focus solely on the fists, or bring into awareness something that is stressing you out in that moment that makes the exercise necessary.

- As you reflect on the stressor, really notice the contraction of your muscles. Feel your fingernails dig into your skin if possible.

- Whenever it feels too uncomfortable to keep holding on, know that you can slowly and mindfully let go at any time.

- Notice your fingers uncurling, and feel the sensation of letting go trickle up your arms and shoulders.

- Simply observe the sensation of letting go.

- Repeat as many times as required until you achieve your desired intention for practicing (e.g., calming down, becoming more present, being able to let go of a stressor for the time being).

FURTHER MODIFICATIONS AND OPTIONS FOR CREATIVITY

o If clenching the fists is too painful or not possible due to context or physical limitations, any muscle group can be clenched and released: the stomach and feet are other popular choices. Many people like to clench the shoulders and raise them toward their ears and then release them with a breath. A few rounds of releasing the shoulders in this way may naturally lead clients to experiment with some of their own stretches or other pleasant expressive movements.

o You can clench and release bilaterally (e.g., first time on the right side, next time on the left side). This practice is also a great way to introduce the concept of bilateral stimulation/dual attention stimulus.

o If clients have a song or series of songs that they associate with letting go, encourage them to play one of those songs as they work with this exercise. There is no shortage of popular songs that can be applied to the holding on/letting go idea.

Consider this case as a model for how the Clench and Release technique may open new perspectives and insights for a client: Cara presented for services to address borderline personality disorder, which she was coming to understand as a manifestation of complex PTSD. Initially afraid of EMDR therapy, Cara was willing to engage in dialectical behavior therapy (DBT) to acquire coping skills and life strategies. When Cara's therapist first showed her the Clench and Release technique, Cara simply refused to let go! After several invitations to release the grip, Cara proclaimed to her therapist, "Come on! You know that holding on to things is part of my problem."

Then Cara started laughing, inspired by the insight she gleaned from this embodied learning. She eventually began to loosen the grip and was open to discussing with her therapist how holding on too tightly to many things in her life—people, relationships, past situations—was keeping her stuck in her turmoil. Cara proposed that doing the Clench and Release exercise every day would help her to practice the art of letting go. Very shortly after this monumental session, Cara expressed her readiness to move into EMDR therapy and had a marvelous experience with it. Toward the termination of her treatment, Cara noted how the DBT helped her with coping and served as a way she could grow to trust her therapist. However, the EMDR therapy is what she needed to truly work through the issues in her life that kept her for over a decade in a perpetual loop of coping alone.

TRANSFORMING DAY-TO-DAY ACTIVITIES INTO MEDITATION

In your clinical practice, you have likely heard clients share insights such as, "I really feel in the zone when I'm vacuuming the carpet" or "Washing the dishes brings me a sense of great peace." For Jan, a woman in long-term recovery from alcoholism who went on to mentor other women in recovery, engaging in practices of daily living with full intention and attention is a vital part of her aftercare. Jan shares:

> When people I sponsor want to learn how to stay present and live in the moment, I tell them to start by doing only one activity at a time. Like if you are going to fold the laundry, focus on folding the laundry. Don't fold the laundry and have dinner going while you listen to the radio and talk on the phone. Just fold the laundry.

In the spirit of "just fold the laundry," try the suggested steps of this exercise:

- Choose one activity that you do every day, no matter what. Some popular options are brushing your teeth, washing your hands, hanging up clothes, making dinner, walking the dog, or taking out the garbage.

- After choosing an activity, set an intention to focus exclusively on that activity as you do it, paying attention to every little detail. For instance, if you choose washing your hands, really pay attention to the temperature of the water. Notice the sensation of the soap moving over your skin. Be aware of how your skin feels after the water takes the soap away. Be present to the experience of turning the faucet to the off position.

- If you normally do the chosen activity on autopilot, see how much you can slow it down to savor the experience.

- To build consistency in the practice, challenge yourself to continue engaging in your chosen activity in this way every time you do it. You may notice some initial frustrations slowing down something you normally put on autopilot, and that is completely to be expected. In the spirit of nonjudgment, simply notice the frustration and then draw your attention back to the activity.

- Continue trying this same general exercise with other activities of daily living.

Further Modifications and Options for Creativity

o If doing the whole activity seems like too much right away, commit to 1 minute of time in the chosen activity.

o Consider keeping a journal, either written or more visually expressive (e.g., sketchbook, drawing pad) to document your experiences. Notice what insights arise as you do so.

o Ask a spouse, partner, or friend to join you in the process, either with the same activity or a different one, and then compare experiences. The intent here is not competitive; the hope is that you can be supportive of each other in this new journey.

This is an exercise where clinicians must be open to working with feedback from clients. The key here is to find something, anything, that a client cannot avoid doing on a daily basis and, within the context of your relationship, propose how that activity can be transformed into a mindfulness practice. Even something like brushing the teeth can work. Think of how many of us do other things when brushing our teeth—organizing items on the counter, picking out our clothes for the day, mediating an argument between kids. What will it mean for you and your clients if you can spend two to three full minutes just brushing your teeth? A radical mindfulness practice indeed!

ENERGETIC MASSAGE

Many people describe the sensation of their brain *hurting*, particularly after an intense psychotherapy session. For others, the challenge is calming down the bouncing brain in the first place. Sometimes, individuals may experience both phenomena during a single session. In this mindful exercise inspired by Qigong and Reiki teachings, you can use the power of your own tactile energy to help give the brain (or any other part of the body) a much-needed massage. This is also an excellent exercise for introducing bilateral stimulation/dual attention stimulus, since you use a bilateral motion to generate the energy. Here are the steps:

• Rub your hands together for at least 30 seconds (you can go longer if you want). Allow your hands to generate some heat!

• Pull your hands apart and bring them to your forehead. There are several variations: You can close your eyes and place the base of your palms over your eyes; let your fingers curl over your forehead to the top of your head. Or, you can rest the base of your palms on your cheeks and extend your fingers around your eyes.

- Settle in, and feel the energy you generated in your hands move into your brain. You do not have to force anything—let the process happen naturally.

- Hold for as long as you like.

- Repeat as many times as required until you achieve your desired intention for practicing (e.g., calming down, becoming more present, being able to let go of a stressor for the time being).

FURTHER MODIFICATIONS AND OPTIONS FOR CREATIVITY

o You can bring the energy from your hands to any part of your body that is feeling tense or anxious. Think about bringing the heat energy from your hands to your chest or stomach if you are noticing any tension or pain. The back of the neck is another helpful position. As a clinician, use your discretion about guiding the clients on where to put their hands. Bringing the hands to certain parts of the body may be triggering, yet encouraging clients to breathe through the discomfort or reminding them that you are there in support can be a way to practice distress tolerance.

o The "cranial hold" position is an option after generating the energy by rubbing your hands. To achieve this, horizontally bring one hand to your forehead and the other hand to the back of your head.

o Consider adding another sense into the process for optimal relaxation, such as meditative music (hearing), or an aromatherapy oil (smell).

Mar struggled with embracing any coping skill exercise as part of his clinical treatment. Mar's preference was to use the 50 minutes of the session simply to talk about the problems encountered during the week, and was hesitant to spend any time working with the past or learning new skills to cope. In Mar's logic, he had to maximize the time with his therapist to be a sounding board for his problems because no one was available in his life to do the same. One day, out of sheer frustration, Mar's therapist suggested that they try the energetic massage before they began talking for the day. The therapist explained that taking just a minute to do this simple exercise might relax the brain just enough so that Mar would not become so flustered when talking about what needed to be addressed. In the observation of Mar's therapist, one minute of energetic massage (about three sets) at the beginning of the session created a path for a more organized "talk therapy" session where Mar was not as flustered. Mar noticed this too, and was willing to start and end each session with the energetic massage technique. Although moving into the reprocessing potential of EMDR therapy never appealed to Mar, based on the goals at the time it proved helpful to be able to latch on to at least one coping skill.

NOODLING: THE ART OF "GOING WITH" ORGANIC, EXPRESSIVE MOVEMENT

Dancer and performer Cornelius Hubbard, Jr., teaches a dance exercise he calls "noodling." Developed while he was studying dance in college, Hubbard would often invoke the spirit of a cooking noodle—asking the body to admire the way a noodle slithers freely and easily, without stress. These are admirable qualities that can teach us a great deal about going with the flow of life. Think of how fun—and potentially beneficial—it could be to take on the role of a noodle. Here are the steps to do just that in this fun, Hubbard-inspired movement exercise (used with permission):

- For optimal benefit, come to your feet (although you can also do this sitting or lying down).

- With your next breath, think of taking on the role of a noodle—begin to loosen up and experience the free movement that can come about when you allow this loosening to take place. Begin with your shoulders, and then let the noodling move through the rest of your body.

- Keep noodling, in a mindful way. If you notice judgment or self-criticism arising, know that those experiences are completely normal. On your next exhale, consider releasing the judgment or criticism.

- When you have given yourself a set amount of time to noodle (it is suggested to start with 3 minutes, although you can noodle for less time to start with), allow yourself to be still for a few moments longer (standing, sitting, or lying down). Notice the stillness following the movement. Observe the energy in your body.

- Repeat as many times as required until you achieve your desired intention for practicing (e.g., calming down, becoming more present, being able to let loose and not judge yourself for the time being).

FURTHER MODIFICATIONS AND OPTIONS FOR CREATIVITY

○ Although you or your clients can do this in silence, it is lots of fun if you put on some music that can bring out your inner noodle! Adding music may help clients anchor in the present if they have a tendency to dissociate. Literally any genre or series of genres can be used for this exercise, although we do recommend something light, effervescent, and bouncy to begin.

○ This exercise can be fun with props such as scarves or ribbons: excellent for children and adults alike!

○ To further orient the experience of bilateral stimulation and being aware of both sides (dual attention stimulus), invite the client to noodle on the right side, then the left. Continue alternating.

In EMDR therapy, never underestimate the power of taking a movement break if the flow of the session at any phase seems to get stuck. Often, taking a short walk outside can help with this process. If going outside is not practical or feasible at your facility, consider how noodling (or some variation of it) can be enrolled for this purpose.

THE EXPRESSIVE ARTS AS MEDITATION

The field of expressive arts therapy stresses the power of healing through multimodal engagement in creative practices. Think about how you can combine dance with poetry writing and follow it up with explorative photography. Another combination could be painting, playlist creation, and making a short film. Although starting with any expressive practice to engage with present moment awareness is excellent, you can practice the art of stepping outside of your comfort zone by engaging in other expressive practices that may seem less organic. The focus of expressive arts work is on process, as opposed to striving or forcing some end product. Here are some steps you can take to experiment with using creativity and expression to explore mindful practice:

• Consider the following expressive arts practices: writing (e.g., journaling, poetry, fiction), painting, sculpting, pottery making, creating collage, dancing/expressive movement, making or listening to music, taking photographs, filmmaking, designing/making clothes. Which of these practices resonates with you the most?

• Gather the necessary materials to engage in the practice.

• Decide on the amount of time that you will set aside to engage in the practice as meditation, and set a timer accordingly.

• Begin practicing your chosen activity with the intention of being totally present. If it is possible to turn off potentially distracting technology, do that.

- If, during the practice, you notice judgment rising up or you find yourself distracted, it does not mean you have failed the practice. Like with seated meditation, if you catch your attention wandering simply bring it back to the activity.

- After the timer goes off, make an intentional pause to simply observe and describe your experience. Setting the timer keeps the activity from being outcome-oriented.

FURTHER MODIFICATIONS AND OPTIONS FOR CREATIVITY

○ Although you are certainly welcome to do only the first part of the practice, moving to another expressive arts practice after your pause to observe and describe makes this a true expressive arts experience! The next practice can be as simple as journaling about the primary practice you selected.

○ To challenge yourself and perhaps continue as a practice in distress tolerance, select the expressive arts activity that most stretches the bounds of your comfort zone. Repeat the same practice using this new activity. Take some time afterward to observe and describe the differences you experienced between the two practices.

○ Continue with the main practice using any combination of the expressive arts practices. Consider guiding clients to make a list of practices that seem to work best for stabilizing and comforting, and a list of practices most effective for challenging them and even moving them to action. Knowing which practices serve which purposes may prove to be valuable information to support clients as they progress in their EMDR therapy journey.

The emphasis on multimodal and intermodal art-making processes distinguishes the formal discipline of expressive arts therapy from other schools of practice, such as art, music, drama, or dance/movement therapy. Expressive arts therapy, by its definition as a discipline, embraces an "all of the above" approach that can serve EMDR therapists well; do not be afraid to think outside the box about what art-making or creative process may assist your clients. With clients who protest that "I am not a creative person," explore what being creative means to them. Chances are they associate the word "creative" with the ability to produce a piece that is radically new and original. In reality, being creative simply means that you are bring something new into existence. With clients, shifting to the word "expressive" may alleviate some of the pressure of describing some of these practices.

TYING IT ALL TOGETHER

The practices covered in this chapter serve as a starter pack for creatively engaging in mindful practices with your clients. Familiarize yourself with these practices and experiment with them before you attempt to use them with clients, and you will be more effective in teaching them as part of EMDR therapy Phase 2, Preparation. Moreover, you will have greater finesse in implementing them as enhanced resourcing strategies or even as interweaves/adjuncts to EMDR reprocessing in Phase 3 through Phase 6. Also consider how the practices covered here can work as strategies in Phase 7, Closure. More insights into the use of these practices in each of the EMDR phases are shared in the applicable chapters.

If you want to even further expand your skill set in the art of using creative avenues in practicing mindfulness and enhancing your clinical repertoire, explore some of the recommendations offered here. There is always something new you can learn as a practitioner of creative mindfulness and as a clinician. One new teaching may resonate in a completely new way. One unique twist on a practice may finally help that practice make sense to you, and you can hopefully pass it along to your clients. The essence of trauma-focused care is to optimally tailor your interventions to clients and their unique needs. Expanding your skill set with mindfulness practices and variations, even as an EMDR therapist, will enhance your ability to individualize care.

QUESTIONS FOR REFLECTION AND PERSONAL PRACTICE

- What was my personal experience with engaging in the practices described in this chapter?

- Do any of the practices in this chapter resonate with me more than others? What does this identified resonance teach me about myself and my journey thus far?

- Do I resist any of the practices in this chapter or find them uncomfortable? What lessons are there to be learned from this resistance and discomfort?

- How can I implement one or more of these practices into my daily life?

- What are my general experiences with and feelings about such concepts as creativity and modification?

RESOURCES FOR FURTHER EXPLORATION

Degges-White, S., & Davis, N. (Eds.). (2017). *Integrating the expressive arts into counseling practice: Theory-based interventions.* New York, NY: Springer Publishing.

Emerson, D., & West, J. (2015). *Trauma sensitive yoga in therapy: Bringing the body into treatment.* New York, NY: W. W. Norton.

Hanh, T. N. (2008). *Mindful movements: Ten exercises for well-being.* Berkeley, CA: Parallax Press.

Marich, J. (2014). *Mindful living coping skills (breath, meditation, and grounding exercises).* Retrieved from http://www.traumamadesimple.com/mindful-living-coping-skills.html

Marich, J. (2015). *Dancing mindfulness: A creative path to healing and transformation.* Woodstock, VT: Skylight Paths Press.

Rappaport, L. (Ed.). (2013). *Mindfulness and the creative arts therapies: Theory and practice.* London, England: Jessica Kingsley Publishers.

Weintraub, A. (2012). *Yoga skills for therapists: Effective practices for mood management.* New York, NY: Norton Professional Books.

5

EMDR Phase 1, Client History—Setting the Tone for Trauma-Focused Services

A MINDFUL APPROACH TO HISTORY

A popular definition of history commonly traced to 18th-century Irish statesman Edmund Burke posits that "History is a pact between the dead, the living, and the yet unborn." Shapiro's (2001) idea of the three-pronged protocol—that past events must be cleared out to alleviate present and future disturbance—reflects some of Burke's wisdom on the implications of exploring history. Healing past trauma can change the course of one's history. Yet to change the course of how one's history will play out in the spirit of living a more adaptive life, clinicians must first discover how individuals entrusted to our care are interpreting the series of past events that led them to our care in the first place. As any historian will attest, interpretation of past events is a major component of the study history. How individuals remember an aspect of their personal history can change as new information is revealed or as messages previously understood about themselves and the world are reprocessed. So many of the people we serve present for services with a personal history colored by negative cognitions and messages obtained through unprocessed experiences of trauma. Considering this principle in and of itself is a major step to becoming more trauma-focused in our delivery of services.

In many areas of clinical culture, the helping professions can use very cold and clinical terms to describe those first few sessions when we get to know someone—*Assessment. Intake. Diagnostic evaluation.* Shapiro opted to name the first phase of the EMDR therapy approach "client history," a description that is ultimately more trauma-focused and mindful than some of these other labels learned in graduate training. Utilizing modern mindfulness adaptations as well as classical Buddhist mindfulness practices in one's own personal and professional practice will provide the necessary mindful presence during history taking and rapport building. If a therapist has a personal mindfulness practice, it becomes easier to maintain nonjudgmental awareness in the office and it helps greatly in being able to transmit those practices to the client in Phase 2, Preparation. Mindfulness guides us from the very beginning of the eight-phase protocol.

This chapter explores the heart and the art of obtaining a client history within the context of EMDR therapy. Some insights are offered on how to sensitively use such tools as the Dissociative Experiences Scale (DES), the Primary Care PTSD Screen, and chronological memories-based inventories shared in other books on EMDR therapy. EMDR therapists are challenged within this chapter, however, to think beyond using screenings or inventory devices. Rather, they are challenged to approach Phase 1, Client History, as a total package. Building the therapeutic relationship, determining clients' goals for treatment, and seeking to understand their presenting issues within the context of their personal history are all imperatives in this phase. Competently addressing these imperatives can result from implementing mindful attitudes and approaches to viewing the client history.

THE PURPOSE OF PHASE 1: DEFINITIONS FROM SHAPIRO AND THE EMDR INTERNATIONAL ASSOCIATION

The standard EMDR therapy—the eight-phase protocol as composed by Shapiro (2001)—is inherently very mindful. However, the technique of the protocol can be daunting to many new learners and the focus of initial learning can shift more to the technical and away from the mindful. Highlighting the mindful essence of the techniques can demystify the EMDR therapy approach. Engaging in this pursuit will help you either feel less intimidated by EMDR therapy, or, if you are seasoned, to approach your practice of EMDR with renewed enthusiasm.

Shapiro's (2001) *Eye Movement Desensitization and Reprocessing: Basic Principles, Protocols, and Procedures* is required reading in training programs approved by the EMDR International Association (EMDRIA) and largely regarded as the seminal text in learning EMDR therapy. Interestingly, Shapiro's language in this relatively early book (first published in 1995, followed by a second edition in 2001) does not yet reflect the evolution to EMDR therapy as a complete approach to psychotherapy. Much of her presentation on Phase 1, Client History, is about screening the client for EMDR appropriateness. In her text, she discusses the importance of covering a number of issues as part of the client history: client readiness, level of rapport, emotional disturbance, stability, life supports, general physical health, office setting, neurological impairment/epilepsy issues, eye problems, addiction issues, legal requirements, systems control, secondary gains, timing, medication needs, and dissociative disorders. She also discusses the vital importance of treatment planning and the idea that EMDR should not occur in a vacuum. Rather, the approach should be directed to address the client's presenting reasons for seeking treatment.

The EMDRIA's (2012) definition of EMDR therapy offers a succinct presentation of Phase 1 that reflects the spirit of Shapiro's initial cautions coupled with recognition of EMDR therapy as a complete system of psychotherapy:

[In] Phase 1, Client History, the clinician begins the process of treatment planning using the concept of incomplete processing and integration of memories of adverse life experiences. The clinician identifies as complete a clinical picture as is prudent before offering EMDR reprocessing. (p. 2)

The rest of the definition nicely translates into a series of tasks offered here in clinically instructive bullet points. For the new EMDR therapist still working through the intricacies of client history and the interplay that may have to occur between Phase 1, Client History, and Phase 2, Preparation, approaching these points as a step-by-step guide may prove useful.

- Determine the suitability of EMDR therapy for the client and for the presenting problem, and decide whether the timing is appropriate.

- Explore targets for future EMDR reprocessing from negative events in the client's life, based on the presenting issue(s).

- Prepare a treatment plan with attention to past and present experiences and future clinical issues.

- Identify positive or adaptive aspects of the client's personality and life experience.

- Postpone completing a detailed trauma history when working with a client with a complex trauma history until the client has developed adequate affect regulation skills and resources to remain stable.

- Address any secondary gain issues that might prevent positive treatment effects.

There is a great deal of finesse involved with approaching Phase 1 as an entry point for client treatment. As Shapiro observes, "EMDR processing is never implemented in the absence of an adequate client history, a clinical relationship that includes rapport and client comfort, adequate client resources, and a treatment plan" (2001, p. 120).

Our essential position is that EMDR therapists who are cultivating some form of a mindfulness practice are more adequately attuned to the care involved in making these required clinical judgment calls. For instance, both the EMDRIA definition and the Shapiro summary of her own chapter suggest that resource building, which EMDR therapists often associate with Phase 2, Preparation, may need to be a part of Phase 1. Another way to look at it is that some Phase 2 work (covered more fully in the next chapter) may need to be implemented into Phase 1, or that Phase 1 elements may need to be revisited after some Phase 2 work is completed.

What we seek to emphasize is that no simple worksheet or series of instruments exist to do a Phase 1 in EMDR therapy. Although these tools may assist, being truly trauma-focused in your delivery of Phase 1 challenges you to approach the phase as you would starting any other treatment—getting to know your client and their inner world. Two major aspects make this principle different in EMDR therapy. First, extrapolating every little detail of narrative from the client about their background is not required, nor is it advised in EMDR therapy. As we will continue to explore in this chapter, approaching a history in that way is not trauma-informed. What we are looking for is a general profile of the client's worldview, existing strengths and resources, the nature of presenting issues, and the role that unhealed trauma played or continues to play in the manifestation of these issues. That is the second feature of an EMDR client history that may distinguish it from many other forms of therapy.

HONOR POSSIBILITIES IN PHASE 1: GATHERING CLIENT HISTORY IN A MINDFUL WAY

Most clinicians coming to us for EMDR therapy training arrive with training in another major therapeutic modality. The skill of completing a clinical intake or initial session is extant. In the initial stages of their learning, new trainees are generally best served by first using EMDR therapy on clients with whom they have already conducted a clinical intake and built rapport. With these clients, therapists can begin to practice obtaining client history in the style of EMDR therapy. For those who are dedicated to practicing EMDR therapy as their primary modality, the two paths—their existing training and the new, EMDR way of approaching history—blend. As a result, those clinicians identifying primarily as EMDR therapists begin to see

Phase 1, Client History, *as* the clinical intake. At Refuge Recovery Centers in Los Angeles, where the entire clinical team is trained in EMDR therapy and EMDR is a primary approach used, the clinical team views all clients coming in to treatment services as EMDR clients in Phase 1 (Dansiger, 2016).

To conduct Phase 1 in a mindful way, it is important that EMDR therapists are first attuned to what it means to conduct clinical intake, as a general concept, in a trauma-sensitive and trauma-responsive manner. These principles are first covered as universal competencies in trauma-focused care (regardless of EMDR therapy training or use). Then, specific suggestions are offered for gathering client history to build the best possible treatment plan for the client. This presentation includes clinical aids that you are free to adopt or work with alongside existing tools in your clinical practice.

BEST PRACTICES FOR CLINICAL INTERACTION

Clinical cultures tend to promote division between the initial intake and the rest of treatment. To truly be trauma-focused and mindful in your practice, it is vital that you see the initial session as part of the treatment. The initial session, which you may already see as the first part of EMDR therapy Phase 1, sets the tone for the rest of treatment. These initial sessions, even more than gathering data, are a time to build the necessary rapport and therapeutic alliance to forge ahead with the other EMDR phases. Consider implementing these best practices into action from your first session with a client and keep them in play during the rest of treatment.

- *Do be genuine and build rapport from the first greeting.* Consider that your first encounter with a client is a chance to begin building this rapport. Do you force clients to shake your hand when you greet them in a lobby or waiting area, or do you ask if it is okay to shake hands? Are you overpowering with your energy and enthusiasm, or can you gauge clients' initial nonverbal feedback that indicates how they feel about being there for that first session? These are all questions that the mindful EMDR therapist must ask of themselves in evaluating their own practice. There are no easy, right-or-wrong answers. Rather, take issues such as these into consideration when building rapport. A solid working definition of sincerity is to show clients the most real, yet compassionate, version of yourself. Clients can generally spot someone who is not genuine a mile away. If you have concerns about this in your own practice, consider seeking additional supervision or consultation.

- *Do not retraumatize.* Clinicians most often retraumatize by prodding for too many details too soon or coming across as interrogatory. Yes, the intake forms that many clinicians are asked to use in their settings seem to promote this prodding and interrogatory style. Accreditation standards under which clinicians work may require us to ask a plethora of questions about past abuse and trauma in this first session before adequate rapport is established. Our general position is that the best clinical intake sessions are conversations that unfold organically. Make getting to know your clients a priority and respect that they may not be comfortable sharing much of their story until they get to know you better. You can use your intake form as a guide for the conversation. For seasoned clinicians, with the assistance of your own breath and commitment to mindful presence, you'll probably find that you are able to jump around your form and get the information you need from the flow of the conversation. For new clinicians, developing this art may take some time. The more committed you as a clinician are to mindful practice, which can include working on developing this art with a consultant or supervisor, the easier this process becomes.

- *Do ask open-ended questions.* Standardized intake forms are notorious for using closed questions (e.g., "Have you ever been sexually abused?") requiring a yes/no answer. Such questions can promote the interrogatory climate that can make clients feel defensive and triggered. Consider how questions that start with the words "what" and "how" generally allow clients to give you as much or as little detail as they are ready to offer. Such questions as "What were things like for you growing up?" "How did that affect you?" "What are things like in your marriage?" "How is that affecting you now?" may yield a treasure trove of information that allows you to fill out your required forms while still giving clients a great amount of control.

- *Do consider that getting an exact, chronological trauma history may be unsafe or impractical because of how the memories are stored in the limbic brain.* Many EMDR clinicians are drawn to the modality recognizing that talk therapy is insufficient to help people heal from trauma. So why would you, as an EMDR clinician, fall into the same traps during your initial meeting with a client that can make talk therapy ineffective? Encouraging clients to share their trauma narrative in early sessions, especially in the absence of affect regulation or other coping skills to ease and balance intense visceral experiences, can overtax the limbic brain. This phenomenon is what can cause many clients to become flooded in the first session, often prompting a decision not to return. Instead of obsessing over chronology, which may not work anyway because memories with high degrees of limbic charge may be accompanied by distortions in rational time, determining presenting issues and corresponding themes is of utmost importance.

- *Do be nonjudgmental.* Being nonjudgmental does not mean you must endorse maladaptive or unhealthy behavior. It does mean that you will respect the dignity of the person at all times. Clients who present for services have a right to be there. There is a high chance that any of these horrible behaviors you hear clients share are rooted in unhealed trauma; consider that the hope offered with the EMDR therapy approach is that we can more compassionately address these individuals. A common axiom in the trauma-informed movement is that trauma-informed care is about what *happened* to you, not what is *wrong* with you. While there may be organic opportunities for challenging clients at various junctures in their treatment journey, tackling a client with overt confrontation in an initial session will generally discourage the client from proceeding with treatment. A major component in this phenomenon is the role that shame plays in many trauma-based presenting issues. *Shame* is when clients internalize those negative cognitions we are all too familiar with in EMDR therapy as core truths about the self. As clinicians, we are in a position of power to help them start seeing that a new truth is possible.

- *Do assure clients that they may not be alone in their experiences.* Many clients presenting for services believe themselves to be uniquely crazy, awful, or defective. You want to avoid saying such things as, "Everyone's felt like that," or "Everyone's been through that," because those can come across as minimizing, patronizing, or otherwise demeaning. However, if you can genuinely share with a client that you have worked with other clients in similar situations and that similar beliefs are shared, you may assist in helping the client to feel more at ease about seeking services. Although it is generally wise to steer away from the phrase "I understand," respecting that no one can ever truly understand what another has been through, if you do relate to an experience shared by a client there is generally little harm in sharing this connection. Please respect, however, your own individual feelings about self-disclosure. Using the statement "I relate" can come across as not genuine if you do not mean it or if you are uncomfortable using it.

- *Do make use of the stop sign when appropriate.* Let people know that they can opt out of answering questions in the history (the only exception may come with questions addressing the possibility of suicide or harm to others). Throughout her work, Shapiro emphasizes use of this technique, generally recommending that clients develop a specific physical gesture that they can use to stop the flow of EMDR. Although EMDR therapists generally associate this technique as most often used during the reprocessing phases, consider the value that it may carry as part of the clinical intake/client history phase.

- *Do be mindful of how you give screening tools or devices to clients.* Be careful to adequately orient the client to the rationale for having them fill out the tool. Also, avoid placing people in a crowded waiting room or small confined office if you determine that those environments may be too triggering/activating. Take this same care in sending clients home with materials; generally, this decision must be made on a case-by-case basis. For instance, the Dissociative Experience Scale (DES), used by many EMDR therapists, is an extensive instrument that can be very helpful in completing Phase 1 and then moving forward. It may take a great deal of time to fill out, and the temptation can be to simply send every client home with it to complete and bring back next time. Some clients can handle this, but others may feel triggered by the questions. Although more time-consuming, you may need to walk clients who present as subjectively less stable through the DES or other instrument in a subsequent session.

- *Do have closure strategies ready.* Allow at least 10 minutes to close any session, especially the first session. One of the greatest errors in clinical treatment is this tendency to run sessions to the very last second without allowing adequate time for closure. In your initial session with a client, consider teaching a brief coping skill toward the end of a session. Any of the skills we covered in the previous two chapters or cited in other resources are excellent candidates for this task. Not only does this promote safety and stabilization, it can also allow your clients to leave their first session with something concrete to try out before the next session. For many clients, completing even a minor task can be empowering. A challenge that many EMDR therapists face is whether to even utter the letters "E-M-D-R" in that first session when a client is not specifically coming to services for that therapy. For some clients, getting some information about the EMDR approach in the form of your explanation or an informational pamphlet may promote hope. For others, getting mired in something that sounds so technical or strange can feel alienating in an initial session. Like many issues in EMDR therapy, a great deal of clinical judgment is involved—judgment that may be honed through your own personal mindfulness practice.

- *Consider that evaluating a client is an ongoing process.* The shift between Phases 2 and 3 in EMDR therapy is another major time to cover issues relevant to evaluation and readiness. This principle of evaluation can apply to trauma therapy in general, as most modalities ask their practitioners to evaluate when a person is sufficiently stable to handle deeper work. More detail on this point of evaluation appears at the beginning of Chapter 7.

Many clinicians enter EMDR training believing that they will get a thorough education on the basics of trauma because EMDR is a modality primarily known as a trauma therapy. However, many training programs in EMDR therapy, although fantastic in quality when teaching the technique of EMDR, spend more training hours on technique and fewer on these vital foundations ubiquitous to trauma care. Many trainees arrive with a solid understanding of trauma, and others have barely been exposed to what trauma-informed, trauma-sensitive, trauma-responsive, or trauma-focused care even means. If you are reading this and still identify largely with the latter, you are advised to deepen your study even further through reading, continuing-education courses, or delving into your own trauma-focused personal therapy with an EMDR therapist. Although you may be able to master the technique of EMDR therapy Phase 1 without this foundation, you will likely find yourself struggling with the art of delivering Phase 1 in a way that optimally serves your clients.

SPECIFIC STRATEGIES FOR PHASE 1, CLIENT HISTORY

HOW TO AVOID BADGERING A CLIENT WITH NARRATIVE

One of the great misconceptions among the general public is that trauma-focused therapy is geared toward talking about what happened to you as a way to move through the pain. As Ben, a newly trained EMDR therapist, recently shared, "What I love about EMDR therapy is that it doesn't badger people with narrative." This statement reflects the spirit of how to approach client history in EMDR therapy. Of course, some talking is required. In general, talking is an activity that human beings use to make connections and collect valuable information. Yet also consider how we clinicians can learn about people from other parts of experience—nonverbal communication, the power of presence, or what in holistic circles is often referred to as *holding space* for someone.

The general approach to take in gathering client history within EMDR therapy can be summarized by these functions:

- *Engaging in general conversation*: getting to know the individual, rapport building, coming to understand reasons for seeking services, assessing for any acute safety risks (e.g., imminent risk to self or others).

- *Recognizing strengths, assets, and recovery capital*: through initial rapport building, asking clients and/or helping them to identify the things they have in their life (both internal and external) that can help them meet their goals.

- *Explaining the general ideals of trauma-focused care*: Many clients present for services have never conceptualized their presenting issues through the lens of trauma; others are well aware that their problems are rooted in trauma; and others still may recognize that while trauma is an issue, they do not want to have a label such as PTSD. Having a conversation about what trauma means and how you use trauma-focused principles in your work can be a valuable part of this first phase of treatment.

- *Identifying goals for services*: Although some clients may not be able to name specific goals during their first session, you can work with just about anything they give you—even a modicum of willingness to engage in a process of discovery.

- *Taking an inventory of key themes, negative cognitions, and potential target memories connected to goals for services*: Within the scope of the therapeutic relationship and determination of client readiness for this process, assist the client in being able to uncover several potential targets for later phases of work in EMDR therapy. We present on the pages that follow a model worksheet we use for this process.

Although these functions can generally be followed in this order, we caution you to use clinical judgment, which can include honoring client readiness and preference, during this process. For instance, some clients may need to learn coping skills or other distress tolerance resources that we ordinarily associate with Phase 2, Preparation, in EMDR therapy before they can engage with you in taking an inventory of themes, negative cognitions, and potential target memories. Moreover, you are also empowered within Phase 1 to developmentally modify how you deliver these essential functions depending on your audience. How you build rapport with a child will differ from how you build rapport with an adult, as an obvious example. There is no shortage of resources within the cannon of EMDR literature on using the phases of EMDR therapy with a variety of populations and how to make necessary modifications to your presentation. Approaching client history using a mindful focus with any of these populations can further ensure your success.

SAMPLE CASE USING WORKSHEETS FOR HISTORY TAKING

Exhibits 5.1 through 5.4 present worksheets to ensure your success as an EMDR therapist committed to becoming more mindful and trauma-focused in the delivery of Phase 1, Client History. Within the flow of this chapter, the worksheets are filled in using a sample case. The same case is revisited in Chapter 9 to demonstrate use of other clinical aids. Clean copies of these clinical aids appear in the appendix and are available online (www.springerpub.com/marich) for use in clinical settings. Feel free to make modifications that may better serve you clinically in your practice of EMDR therapy.

EXHIBIT 5.1 Phase 1, Client History Taking—General Functions for Success

Insights from general initial conversations, clinical intake, rapport building (you can supplement with any clinical intake forms you are asked to use in your place of employment):

Sandy (client) has been through several therapies and a number of treatments. Client shows openness and hope about EMDR. Sandy reports many adverse life events and two or three significant traumas. Sandy reports issues related to sexual orientation and coming-out process. Sandy has good insight into these issues, and sees them as targets for reprocessing. Sandy has been sober three years and is committed to recovery.

Strengths, assets, recovery capital and resources:
- *Regular attendance at AA meetings*
- *New interest in mindfulness*
- *Two close friends*
- *Enjoys art and music; plays in a band*
- *Compassionate*
- *Reads spiritual literature*

Goals for services (general or specific):
- *Start and maintain romantic relationships*
- *Rethink/repurpose career goals*
- *Reduce anger reactivity*
- *Increase intimacy*
- *Reduce self-hating self-talk*
- *Improve boundaries with parents*

Client's general understanding of trauma and response to initial education about trauma-focused care:

Client is new to idea of trauma and trauma focus. Client claims to be open to it, and responded well to the scientific theoretical explanation of EMDR therapy. Client did outside reading that increased openness, and increased insight into institutional forms of trauma.

EXHIBIT 5.2 Phase 1, Client History Taking—Identifying Themes, Negative Cognitions, and Potential Targets

Going through a detailed, chronological history is not vital. Recounting a detailed history may be impossible until you have processed certain memories, or you may not feel ready for it right now. The imperative is to identify themes that are linked to presenting issues:

Theme 1 (Connected to Presenting Issue): *Anger and reactivity*
Negative Cognition: *I am not in control.*

- First floatback memory: *Bullying in elementary school due to sexual orientation*
- Worst floatback memory: *Age 13, sudden death of beloved cousin*
- Most recent floatback memory: *Friend in AA overdosed and hospitalized*

Theme 2 (Connected to Presenting Issue): *Romantic relationships*
Negative Cognition: *I cannot trust anyone.*

- First floatback memory: *Age 6, bullied at new school of mother's choosing*
- Worst floatback memory: *College significant other disclosed cheating*
- Most recent floatback memory: *Most recent dating situation ended over text*

Theme 3 (Connected to Presenting Issue): *Boundaries with parents*
Negative Cognition: *I have to be perfect.*

- First floatback memory: *Age 8, client asked why he got a "B" on report card*
- Worst floatback memory: *Mother's inappropriate use of client as confidante*
- Most recent floatback memory: *Public shaming by father about career plans*

NOTES: (a) Not required to fill out all three (depends on client presentation) or you may use additional pages, if needed; (b) Use the negative cognitions list with instructions on the opposite page to help you if client is not able to readily identify themes and corresponding cognitions independently.

EXHIBIT 5.3 Phase 1, Client History Taking—The "Greatest Hits" List of Negative Cognitions

Responsibility
I should have known better.
I should have done something.
I did something wrong.
I am to blame.
I cannot be trusted.

Safety
I cannot trust myself.
I cannot trust anyone.
I am in danger.
I am not safe.
I cannot show my emotions.

Choice
I am not in control.
I have to be perfect/please everyone.
I am weak.
I am trapped.
I have no options.

Power
I cannot get what I want.
I cannot handle it/stand it.
I cannot succeed.
I cannot stand up for myself.
I cannot let it out.
I am powerless/helpless.

Value
I am a bad person/I am terrible.
I am permanently damaged.
I am defective.
I am worthless/inadequate.

How to Use:
- Have your client check off any negative beliefs that may still be held in the present, especially those that go along with the chosen presenting issue.
- If more than three are checked, have client go over the list again to rank (1, 2, 3) the "hottest" or "most charged" beliefs.
- Once identified, ask client three floatback questions and document on the corresponding worksheet:

Looking back over the course of your life, when is the **first** *time you believed . . . (e.g., I am . . .; I cannot . . .; I do not . . .)*

Looking back over the course of your life, when is the **worst** *time you believed . . .*

Looking back over the course of your life, when is the **most recent** *time you believed . . .*

(continued)

EXHIBIT 5.3 Phase 1: Client History Taking—The "Greatest Hits" List of Negative Cognitions (*continued*)

I am insignificant.
I am not important.
I deserve to die.
I deserve only bad things.
I am stupid.
I do not belong.
I am different.
I am a failure.
I am ugly.
My body is ugly.
I am alone.

EXHIBIT 5.4 Case Conceptualization and Treatment Plan

Directions: Use as many of these pages as you need throughout your engagement with the client. Part of Phase 8, Reevaluation, is to be continuously evaluating the treatment plan, writing new goals and objectives, and developing targets and future templates accordingly.

Presenting Issue: *Anger and Reactivity*

Goal and Desired Objectives:
Decrease anger reactivity and increase distress tolerance by learning new anger management tools and learning use of mindfulness and loving kindness; will result in what client describes as a more peaceful existence.

EMDR Preparation Resources, Targets, or Future Templates to Address:

- *Preparation: Mindfulness training, moving meditation practices, continued engagement in AA meetings*
- *RDI protocol to identify internal resources specific to anger management*
- *Targets: Ongoing bullying in school, the sudden death of their cousin*
- *Future templates: Work, dating, and driving situations*

Presenting Issue: *Romantic difficulties*

EXHIBIT 5.4 Case Conceptualization and Treatment Plan (*continued*)

Goal and Desired Objectives:
Increase ability to establish and maintain emotional intimacy by learning and testing out new communication skills and learning use of mindfulness and loving kindness; will result in decreased fear of vulnerability in relationships.

EMDR Preparation Resources, Targets, or Future Templates to Address:

- *Preparation: Mindfulness training; Loving Kindness practice; continued engagement in AA meetings and working with sponsor on this matter*
- *RDI protocol to identify internal resources specific to intimacy*
- *Targets: Relationship to their mother, previous dating experiences*
- *Future templates: Visualization of future dating scenarios*

Presenting Issue: *Boundaries with parents*

Goal and Desired Objectives:
Complete separation and individuation from parents through increasing assertiveness and learning use of mindfulness and loving kindness; develop separate relationships with mother and father

EMDR Preparation Resources, Targets, or Future Templates to Address:

- *Preparation: Mindfulness training, walking meditation, expressive arts; explore potential of working with another recovery fellowship like Al-Anon or Refuge Recovery to address unhealthy attachment issues*
- *RDI protocol to identify internal resources specific to increasing assertiveness*
- *Targets: Mother's inappropriateness, early childhood experiences leading to need to be perfect*
- *Future templates: Visualization of future family events and phone calls*

Presenting Issue: *Impact of bullying due to sexual orientation (revealed as a separate presenting issue for focus during initial history taking/cognitions inventory)*

Goal and Desired Objectives:
Integrate experience of coming-out process and current self-identity through identifying supportive people and institutions to grow identity related to sexual orientation; will allow for an increase in positive self-talk

(continued)

EXHIBIT 5.4 Case Conceptualization and Treatment Plan (*continued*)

and enable development of healthy communication about social justice issues.

EMDR Preparation Resources, Targets, or Future Templates to Address:

- Preparation: Mindfulness training; Loving Kindness practice; expressive arts; explore possibility of attending an LGBT-specific 12-step meeting
- RDI protocol to identify internal resources specific to increasing assertiveness
- Targets: Negative/oppressive cognitions of "I am not safe in this world" and "I am defective" learned from specific bullying incidents and societal messages
- Future templates: Visualization of living an adaptive life with an integrated identity

(Use additional copies of this worksheet if needed)

There are a few pieces of guidance to share about using these styles of worksheets in clinical settings. Although they are not scripts per se, they can help organize your thinking as you embark on a mindful journey through EMDR therapy with your clients. In general, these worksheets should not be used for clients as take-home exercises. Rather, they are designed for you to review with the client within the scope of your therapy sessions.

Many EMDR consultants are full of cautionary tales about sending clients home too early with too much history-taking work. You may have already had the experience of giving a classic EMDR "client guidebook" to an individual with complex trauma. Although clients may respond well to initial conversation, rapport building, and even some rudimentary stabilization exercises, the guidebook exercises can prove too much for clients to complete on their own. One such popular exercise challenges clients to list 10 positive memories and 10 negative memories (a technique Shapiro references in her text and many others also use in history taking). Listing the memories may cause a great deal of dissociation and affective overwhelm. Be cautious about what you send clients home with to work on in between sessions, especially early in the treatment process. A general point of guidance is to have clients work on experimenting with basic mindfulness approaches and coping strategies in between sessions (which can cause their own concerns, which we handle in the next chapter).

The inventory material of Phase 1, for most clients, is best completed in sessions within the context of the compassionate support that you, as the clinician, can provide.

TYING IT ALL TOGETHER

The strategy recommended in this chapter for unearthing potential targets is a solid method for uncovering enough of the history to know how to steer the ship of treatment. However, exploring potential targets in this fashion is less overwhelming than having clients chronologically inventory their life in the style of more narrative approaches. The approach presented in this chapter is more trauma-informed than the list of 10 worst memories, which promotes thinking in chronological terms about issues that may be too messy and disorganized to conceptualize in this manner. Forcing the process of making a neat list can also yield a great deal of frustration.

The major advantage to exploring potential targets for reprocessing using the strategy offered in this chapter is that it directly corresponds to a standard treatment plan. The treatment plan worksheet that appears on the previous pages ought to look like a standard issue treatment plan used by many treatment centers and agencies in North America. The presenting issue for treatment generally corresponds to a theme and negative cognition from which several potential targets (including what Shapiro calls a touchstone memory) can be unearthed. These targets can be placed on the treatment plan under general intervention (EMDR therapy) to offer a specific course of action within the remaining phases of EMDR therapy. This treatment plan also recommends that you use the existing information given to you by the client on strengths and resources to begin building the preparation components. An inventory of what else may need to be explored and strengthened in the preparation phase can also be reflected on this treatment plan. The future template component of a treatment plan, which may at first glance seem like jumping too far ahead in Phase 1, directly corresponds with goals presented for services. The mindful EMDR therapist respects the core Shapiro (2001) teaching that the purpose of EMDR is to help an individual live a more adaptive life. So why wouldn't you be thinking ahead in the treatment plan about what that can look like for a client?

The treatment plan is open to change and adaptation as the course of the EMDR therapy flows from client to client. Yet it is necessary to appreciate how the structure can help you with the overall artistic vision for what EMDR can do. Doing this mindfully takes many forms. Mindfulness encourages us to become more aware of moment-to-moment experience, noticing that all things are impermanent and that the only permanent thing we will ever find is change. Here, clinicians can see our history taking and treatment planning in this dynamic light. Moment to moment, the history we are witnessing with our clients is changing. Minute by minute, clients are leading us through the tangled yarn of their experience. Session by session, clarity grows, new insights develop, resources build, and the potential for reprocessing grows. Client by client, the adventure that is the innate healing abilities of each individual is made manifest. All of this is both a function and an outgrowth of mindfulness on the part of both the therapist and client. Intake and client history becomes anything but cold and clinical: it is the intricate beginning of the journey.

QUESTIONS FOR REFLECTION AND PERSONAL PRACTICE

- What is your personal, working definition of "history"?
- What does history mean to you?
- What struggles have you experienced thus far as an EMDR therapist in working with Phase 1, Client History?
- How can you see yourself implementing some of the strategies offered in this chapter into your clinical practice?

REFERENCES

Dansiger, S. (2016, August 27). *Mindfulness and the 8-phase protocol as a template for addictions treatment*. Paper presented at the 21st EMDRIA Conference, Minneapolis, MN.

EMDR International Association. (2012). *EMDRIA definition of EMDR*. Austin, TX: Author. Retrieved from http://c.ymcdn.com/sites/www.emdria.org/resource/resmgr/Definition/EMDRIADefinitionofEMDR.pdf

Shapiro, F. (2001). *Eye movement desensitization and reprocessing: Basic principles, protocols, and procedures* (2nd ed.). New York, NY: Guilford Press.

6

EMDR Phase 2, Preparation in Trauma-Focused Care

MINDFULLY NAVIGATING THE PREPARATION PHASE

Consultees in EMDR therapy consistently pose these questions:

- How much preparation is considered sufficient in Phase 2, Preparation?

- How do clinicians know when a client is truly ready to plunge into the deeper work of trauma reprocessing in Phases 3 through 6?

- How stable does a client really have to be in order to manage these trauma-reprocessing components that many see as the heart of EMDR therapy?

If you gathered 10 EMDR consulting therapists around a conference table, it's very likely you would get 10 different answers to these questions. Many believe, especially in working with complex trauma, that the reprocessing phases of EMDR therapy ought not to commence until a person is adequately stabilized. Others follow Dr. Francine Shapiro's caution to the letter, as noted in her 2001 work, *Eye Movement Desensitization and Reprocessing: Basic Principles, Protocols, and Procedures,* that preparation is not processing, and believe that the real work of EMDR cannot be achieved until traumatic memories are targeted. A popular literature review conducted by a team that included many EMDR therapists challenged long-held recommendations by the 2012 International Society for Traumatic Stress Studies

(ISTSS) expert task force (Cloitre et al., 2012) for the implementation of an extensive stabilization phase with complex posttraumatic stress disorder (PTSD) survivors (De Jongh et al., 2016). This research review concluded that (a) there is no substantive research base for the task force's recommendations for such an extensive period of stabilization, and (b) complex PTSD survivors are better served by more trauma-focused treatments, even though there is some risk involved. Refined clinical judgment is imperative in managing that risk.

Navigating the intricacies of preparation involves much more finesse than making sure clients can get to a Calm Safe Place. In contrast, Phase 2 does not suggest that a client must achieve a perfect state of stabilization to handle the reprocessing phases of EMDR therapy (Phases 3–6). Many therapists are reluctant to take clients into these post-preparation phases, fearing they are not stable enough to handle them. In stymieing the flow of EMDR therapy out of their own fear and trepidation, clinicians may be preventing their clients from getting the help they need via processing to become more stable. It's noteworthy that Shapiro chose the word "preparation" in naming Phase 2 instead of "stabilization," the word used in the consensus model of trauma treatment referenced by the ISTSS task force tracing to the early work of Pierre Janet. Stabilization is a big word that sets a high standard. Preparation, deriving from the Latin *praeparare*, meaning "to make ready beforehand," truly focuses on the aspect of readiness. Consider how the questions that opened this chapter might look if clinicians embraced the challenge to engender readiness in their clients:

- What activities do I have to engage in with my clients to get them ready for trauma reprocessing?

- What kind of tone needs to be established in our therapeutic relationship?

- What other factors of living must be at least addressed (e.g., living situation, nature of support, secondary gains) to help the client and therapist feel more secure about taking a journey into the later phases?

As a foundation, Phase 2, Preparation, must include introducing clients to mindfulness practice—this core assumption informs the chapter. Such training can allow clients to enhance their coping skill repertoire, build internal resources, and widen their affective window of tolerance. Special attention is paid to the role that cultivating mindfulness practices can play in heightening distress tolerance. Allowing for this practice in the Preparation phase will allow for successful trauma reprocessing in the later phases of the protocol. The information offered in this chapter guides both seasoned EMDR therapists and those who are newly learning EMDR in how they can deliver EMDR Phase 2, Preparation, in a more trauma-focused manner by attending to it mindfully.

A TRAUMA-FOCUSED APPROACH TO PREPARATION

The Broader Context for Healing Trauma

In his landmark work *The Body Keeps the Score*, Dr. Bessel van der Kolk (2014) asserts, "For real change to take place, the body needs to learn that the danger has passed and to live in the reality of the present" (p. 21). Van der Kolk expounds three key pathways to intervention that can help survivors of trauma feel alive in the present and live a more adaptive, transformed life:

- *Top-down methods:* talking, connecting with others, self-knowledge,

- *Technology:* medications to shut down inappropriate alarm reactions; other therapies/technologies that change the way the brain organizes information, and

- *Bottom-up methods:* allowing the body to have experiences that deeply and viscerally contradict the helplessness, rage, and collapse that result from the trauma

Many clinicians operate from only one of the pathways to intervention, all of which correspond with MacLean's (1990) triune model of the brain. For instance, clinicians whose main skill set involves helping clients to talk out their problems, develop a support network, and acquire a mountain of psychoeducational knowledge about what ails them are primarily working with the neocortex (i.e., the more rational brain unique to primates). In the field of addiction recovery, many programs believe that this "top down" style of intervention is enough. However, much of the damage caused by unprocessed trauma affects the lower brain (i.e., the limbic/mammalian brain and the brain stem). Thus, the styles of intervention Van der Kolk describes as technology and bottom-up methods are also required for total healing to take place. He emphasizes that a combination of all three styles of intervention is needed for optimal healing to occur.

EMDR therapy encompasses all three pathways to intervention. This chapter addresses how the trauma-processing phases of the EMDR standard protocol bring about deep visceral experiences that can contradict and transform trauma's legacy in the body (Phases 3–6). Some of the preparation skills described in this chapter can initiate the process of healing at this bottom-up level. At the very least, engagement in these exercises can help to strengthen or frontload more adaptive material. In EMDR therapy, maladaptive material links with adaptive material for successful processing to occur.

Some clients arrive at EMDR therapy with more adaptive material than do others. The absence or dearth of adaptive material and experiences does not rule out further phases of the EMDR journey; it does mean that more time will need to be spent in Phase 2, Preparation, engaging in what Shapiro calls "frontloading." Quite literally, frontloading is the practice of helping clients acquire healthy, adaptive, or transformative experiences, even something as simple as finally connecting with a deep cleansing breath, in the Preparation phase. Teaching mindfulness skills as part of Phase 2 enhances the process of frontloading, which, according to Shapiro, allows for greater generalization effects in the latter phases of EMDR therapy. The specific skills of mindfulness, whether or not bilateral stimulation is used in Phase 2, can be an active ingredient in both bottom-up healing and top-down healing. A commitment to being mindful in your personal practice can help you more strongly attend to the therapeutic relationship you establish with your clients, a vital aspect of both bottom up and top down healing.

Filling Out the Missing Pieces

RESOURCE DEVELOPMENT AND INSTALLATION

In 2012, Stephen Dansiger conducted a series of short video interviews with Dr. Andrew Leeds regarding EMDR therapy. In one of these videos, Dr. Leeds described the genesis and the history of the Resource Development and Installation (RDI) protocol, which has often been called the "missing piece" of Shapiro's original standard protocol (Dworkin, 2005; Korn & Leeds, 2002; Sonoma Psychotherapy Training Institute, 2012). Leeds described how this protocol developed out of a series of treatment failures, particularly with one client. This complex client would go into what Leeds called a "shame meltdown" every time they went into the standard reprocessing.

The client came into session one day and described a positive image she had in a dream, the type of positive image the client had previously been unable to identify, let alone hold onto. Leeds asked her if she wanted to try and "install" that image using slow passes of eye movements. The client agreed and the results were very positive. Over the course of about 45 minutes, they installed other positive images and beliefs. In a sense, they were frontloading the experience of the Installation phase of the standard protocol, since the client could not get there through standard reprocessing. When the client returned the next week, Leeds found her "almost unrecognizable." The gains included improved sleep, abatement of physical symptoms, and greatly reduced anxiety. Perhaps most importantly, after this successful foray into installing the positive, they returned to the work of trying to reprocess the client's trauma. As a result of their resourcing, the standard protocol went smoothly, bolstered by this new foundation of positive neural networks.

Leeds (2016) insists that the protocol itself has its roots in the work of others, but that he did in fact take it out of its fragmented state and its focus on specific populations (such as Ron Martinez helping children to visualize themselves as superheroes) and solidified it into the form of a now widely used protocol. Leeds contacted Shapiro and suggested he would like to teach this method in advanced EMDR trainings. Shapiro suggested that its success may have been unique to Leeds's skill set, so they agreed to have other EMDR institute trainers try it out. Those other trainers reported the same positive results. It was formalized into a protocol, and the case that began it all was documented in Philip Manfield's *EMDR Casebook* (2003).

Like the Preparation and Closure work suggested by Shapiro with Calm Safe Place, Light Stream, and Container, the RDI protocol (Leeds, 2016) uses visualization as its driving force. Internal resources are identified, and then four types of manifestations of these resources are visualized: mastery resources, role models, coaches, and symbolic/metaphorical resources. Mastery resources are those events or phases of life where the client was able to access and act upon those resources. Role models are those people who represent the successful manifestation of those resources. They do not have to know the person; it could even be a fictional character or a public figure. Coaches are those people who also display those resources and would be helpful if they were right there in the moment, encouraging and coaching the client. Finally, symbolic or metaphorical manifestations are identified, for instance, a tree, which represents strength and flexibility in the way it moves with the wind but has strong roots. All of these are visualized and strengthened using slow, short sets of bilateral stimulation. Two versions of the RDI protocol can be found in Leeds's 2016 *A Guide to the Standard EMDR Therapy Protocols for Clinicians, Supervisors, and Consultants*, Second Edition (pp. 371–375). While Parnell (2007, 2013) and others have adjusted some of the language around what may be visualized, for the most part the flow of the protocol has remained the same: discover new resources and identify already existing ones; visualize one identified resource; strengthen with slow, short sets of bilateral stimulation; and be open to more adaptive responses in the visualization and continue to strengthen those as needed.

The discovery of the wisdom of frontloading resources, and the development of the RDI protocol to allow for clients to titrate their way into reprocessing through building the positive, opens the door to an almost endless variety of resources. Much like we have suggested that Calm Safe Place, Light Stream, and Container are not necessarily enough, RDI and its visualization emphasis contain only part of the story. Mindfulness skills can be fundamental elements of the resourcing picture that allow clinicians to work with more than just the visual domain.

Using the Four Foundations of Mindfulness, a primary teaching of the Buddha, clinicians can witness how this might be implemented. Mindfulness of the body allows clients to become more aware and more connected with their present time experience. Mindfulness of feeling tone, where all experience is seen as pleasant, unpleasant, or neutral, can simplify and balance out the extreme edges of the client's experience. Mindfulness of mind and mindfulness of dharmas (conceptual thought) can be utilized to resource a client when applied from a positive direction. For instance, a client can be guided through the Heart Practices, which allow the client to access and install the resources of Loving Kindness, Compassion (for self and others), Appreciative Joy, and Equanimity. Clinicians can use their own mindfulness practice and clinical judgment to assess which of these mindfulness skills would most resonate with and be successfully installed with each client.

One of the keys to helping our clients to identify and develop their internal resources is our own commitment as clinicians to our own practice of mindfulness. Our own practice serves as a resource through our modeling its practice and benefits, as well as through whatever psychoeducation we need to provide in order for the client to understand and pursue mindfulness skills. Another reason for developing further mindfulness for ourselves is that we can maintain a deeper sense of presence in the therapy room. Mindful attunement to the client's experience will result in more skilled judgment as to what type and degree of resourcing our clients will need in order to prepare for reprocessing. That mindful presence brings us to the next missing link: the relational elements of EMDR therapy.

THE RELATIONAL IMPERATIVE IN EMDR THERAPY

Shapiro (2001) teaches that EMDR therapy is an interaction between client, clinician, and method. In his landmark work, Mark Dworkin (2005) went a step further by proposing that relational issues between client and clinician often impact whether EMDR therapy results are positive or negative. The vital role of the therapeutic relationship as a mechanism of change within larger psychotherapy has been long established (Duncan, Miller, Wampold, & Hubble, 2009). Dworkin's work continued with a paper (along with Nancy Errebo) offering EMDR clinicians direct suggestions for how to repair breaches in the therapeutic relationship; in other words, how to attend to the relationship when the client senses something has gone wrong (Dworkin & Errebo, 2010). EMDR is now regarded as a distinct approach to psychotherapy, rather than a simple technique. Thus, it is important that we EMDR therapists regard this larger truth of the field—the transformative power of the relationship as an element in the change process—and integrate it into our work with EMDR clients.

Attending to relational matters is an important component of laying the groundwork in Phases 1 and 2. Having this strong foundation will serve your client throughout the remaining phases of EMDR therapy, particularly

when it comes to navigating difficult clinical decisions around case conceptualization. In Marich's qualitative phenomenological study investigating
how EMDR therapy was implemented as part of addiction continuing care
with women (2010, 2012), the participants contributed a wealth of thematic
insight into the role of the relationship with their EMDR therapy. The women
who described initially negative experiences with their EMDR therapist used
words/phrases like *rigid, scripted, unclear,* and *not comfortable with trauma
work* to describe the therapists. The two women who had these unfortunate
experiences found their opinions about EMDR and how it worked for them
transformed as soon as they switched to a new therapist. They described the
new therapist using words like *natural, wonderful, intuitive, smart,* and *having
good common sense.* Consider how embracing a commitment to mindfulness
and a mindful approach to EMDR therapy can assist you, as a clinician, in
cultivating these qualities.

NECESSARY SKILLS FOR PREPARATION AND THE ART OF MODIFYING THEM

NO SUCH THING AS "ONE SIZE FITS ALL"

There is no such thing as a simple set of steps you need to follow to perfectly
complete EMDR therapy Phase 2. The EMDRIA (2012) definition of EMDR
therapy is open to a great deal of clinical finesse, depending on the needs of
the client. According to the definition, the key aspects to cover in Phase 2 are:

- Orienting the client to EMDR therapy sufficiently so client can give informed consent.

- Establishing a therapeutic relationship to give the client a sense of
  safety and foster the client's ability to tell the therapist what they're experiencing throughout the reprocessing.

- Developing mastery of skills in self-soothing and in affect regulation
  as appropriate to facilitate dual awareness during the reprocessing sessions and to maintain stability between sessions.

- Promoting the development and expansion of positive and adaptive
  memory networks, thus expanding the window of affect tolerance, and
  stimulating the development of the capacity for relationship (especially
  critical for complex trauma).

The definition also cautions that some clients may need lengthier preparation than others, especially if more frontloading of adaptive material is
needed.

To achieve these key aspects of Phase 2 in our delivery of EMDR therapy, clients ought to learn skills for affect regulation and expanding distress tolerance that can be grouped into these major categories:

- Mindfulness and grounding strategies
- Breathing strategies
- Visualization and multisensory soothing
- Movement, expressive arts, and identification of other recovery capital

In the pages that follow each category is covered, with attention to issues of implementation. A major part of implementation is knowing how to modify the exercises when clients tell you, "I can't meditate; I can't sit still," or "Breathing makes me more anxious." In covering each category, skills covered in previous chapters are referenced, and some new material is shared in this chapter.

The depth and breadth of preparation material can include skills that do or do not directly work with slow bilateral stimulation/dual attention stimulus. For guidelines on applying bilateral stimulation to the various skills as a resource, which will be important for at least some of these skills before moving into the later phases of EMDR therapy, refer to the earlier section in this chapter on RDI (Leeds, 2016). Once you and your client come to understand the value of slow bilateral stimulation as a mechanism for strengthening adaptive connections to resources, you discover that literally anything adaptive can be strengthened, tapped in, toned in, or locked in using eye movements. For some clients, the bilateral stimulation can overwhelm at first. You may be better served to first teach the skills as they are written, without any stimulation. If the client shows a good response, you can integrate slow bilateral movements or another dual attention stimulus for strengthening. Other clients may require the bilateral components to engage with the exercise. Get accustomed to gathering feedback from the clients about which style or combination of skill styles is working for them and be prepared to adapt your preparation plan accordingly.

Mindfulness and Grounding Strategies

Van der Kolk (2014) makes a powerful case for how mindfulness practice can benefit survivors of trauma. He notes that traumatized people are often afraid of feeling, and that mindfulness practices can help orient them to and ease them into this process by widening the sensory experience. Practicing mindfulness can be calming to the sympathetic nervous system, lessening the destruction of fight/flight responses. Mindfulness practices also help to promote distress tolerance as awareness develops that emotional states constantly shift. Hopefully, if you are already an EMDR therapist, you are connecting some dots about how teaching these skills in advance of trauma reprocessing may allow for these phases to progress more smoothly (Phases 3–6).

A significant skill cultivated through mindfulness practice is that of grounding, which literally and figuratively challenges us to find a foundation and be able to remain there. If individuals are unable to remain there, through practice, they can learn to return there. Having a workable set of grounding skills is particularly important when treating dissociative clients or those with complex trauma. If a client can continue to stay grounded in the trauma reprocessing phases of EMDR, they will be much more likely to stay within their affective window of tolerance and not push themselves too far with their reprocessing. In the event abreactions or other elements of reprocessing take an unexpected turn, being able to return to a grounding element at any time throughout the session is crucial. Remember the age-old axiom that an ounce of prevention is worth a pound of cure? Frontloading clients with as many skills as possible defines proactive prevention in EMDR therapy.

For orientation to many of the classic skills within the tradition of mindfulness, please refer to Chapter 3. Clients may balk at learning some of these skills. Many clinicians are tempted at this juncture to abandon the interventions as not working. Please do not give up so easily. Recall, if you can, the frustrations you've personally experienced when learning something new. From this place of lived experience, you can genuinely share on how you've dealt with working through frustrations in your own practice. People can set themselves up to fail with meditating because they are transfixed with some perfect picture, fresh off the cover of *Time* magazine, about what meditation "should" look like. As people, we think that if we can't get to that perfect stillness, we're not really meditating. If you've explored the book to this point and have explored some of the practices, you know that nothing can be further from the truth. The practice of mindfulness is not about clearing your mind or staying perfectly still; the practice is about returning to the moment or to the object of your focus when the attention wanders. Something as simple as clarifying client expectation about what meditation even means can inspire the client to give the practices another attempt.

In trauma-focused care, modifications can always be made. If the time parameter that you, as the clinician, suggest for a practice seems too long, shorten the length of the practice. Some tips on how to do this are offered in Chapters 3 and 4. Also remember that developing consistent practice is more important than developing a lengthy one. If a certain practice doesn't particularly resonate with a client or they are struggling in despair, consider sharing a mindfulness practice in another style.

Breathing Strategies

Several specific breath practices from the yogic traditions are covered in Chapter 4. They can be integrated throughout the phases of EMDR therapy as a resource for clients. So often in EMDR therapy clinicians say things like, "Take a deep breath," especially when checking in for content during the later phases of EMDR therapy. Even this task can be tricky for clients if they've not yet moved passed holding their breath as a protective response. Steady breathing can assist in expanding a client's affective window of tolerance. However, there is an art to teaching clients how to become more comfortable with their breath and to use it in the service of their recovery. Recognize that connecting with the breath in such a way can be much easier said than done for our clients who have been living in a state of hyperarousal.

DEMONSTRATING HYPERAROUSAL AND RELEASE

- Try something—if it's physically available to you, go ahead and squeeze your shoulders up toward your ears. See how long you can hold them there.

- Notice what is happening to your breath as you tense your shoulders in this manner. It's very likely that the breath is shallow or short.

- Now go ahead and release the clench in your shoulders and notice immediately what happens to the breath.

This simple exercise demonstrates how much the breath can be affected by living in hyperarousal. It's often useful to take clients through this exercise if they ask you why doing breath work is so important to the healing process. Do not push, and remember that critical modifications for working with people too overwhelmed with breath are noted in Chapters 3 and 4. Clinicians must be mindful of teaching the practices in a way that pays special attention to how the practices themselves may be vulnerable or triggering. The notion that breath can be both a trigger and a resource is a central teaching in trauma-informed yoga. Many of the practices that we suggest throughout this book can be both a trigger and a resource, especially if modifications are not offered and if you do not work with client feedback.

Allowing for variability in time spent in practices is crucial. Also consider how being in silence for too long may be more distressing for certain clients. In our experience, people have different preferences on how much verbal instruction they may require during a meditation or a guided visualization. Sometimes clients will beg clinicians—in a very polite way, of course—to shut up if we are getting too wordy with leading one of our favorite exercises. It's a good practice to get feedback from a client about whether or not they want more or less of your verbal instruction during an exercise. For many clients, the sound of your voice can be anchoring and assuring whereas being in silence for too long can trigger distress. Another safety tip is that if you are leaving clients in silence for any length of time, let them know how long they are going to be in silence (e.g., "For the next minute verbal instruction will stop") or in an exercise (e.g., "Let's try six full inhales and exhales on this breath"). Finally, always assure your clients that closing their eyes is optional. Many clients get overly distressed when they are in the literal dark for too long, even if closing the eyes may have some benefits for promoting relaxation. In some meditation traditions, it's advised to keep the eyes open, and following this lead is a solid best practice for introducing mindfulness skills and breath work to clients.

Multisensory Soothing

Shapiro and other writers on EMDR therapy have long favored guided visualization techniques for preparation, particularly the Calm Safe Place. Having one Calm Safe Place for a client to retreat is rarely adequate preparation, especially in cases of complex trauma. More importantly, EMDR clinicians must also consider that the Calm Safe Place exercise has a potential to be triggering for clients. In many EMDR trainings, clinicians are advised to help their clients choose a place that does not have people involved to minimize some of this triggering, although this can be difficult to avoid. For some clients, the disruptive or distressing elements just appear, even if clients start with every intention of using the exercise for soothing. Also consider that the Calm Safe Place exercise is a form of intentional dissociation. The exercise advises people to go to a place outside of themselves and the present moment. Clearly, it is not the most mindful skill to use. The Calm Safe Place skill can be useful with certain clients in certain contexts. However, if you are going to implement it with regularity, have other grounding exercises at your disposal for bringing people back into the present if the distress is heightened by the Calm Safe Place. While all preparation exercises run the risk of going awry and potentially serving as experiences for practicing distress tolerance, having the grounding anchor as a safeguard is advised.

In brainstorming potential anchors for grounding or other ways to promote adaptive self-soothing, think outside of the guided visualization box. Although many guided visualizations incorporate other sensory elements, why not actually bring in other sensory elements if they are available? Consider the use of textural elements like rocks, stones, and marbles. In the Preparation phase you can guide a client through a meditation, paying attention to the texture as the primary anchor of focus. Many clients have reported benefit from holding on to their rock, stone, or marble in the later phases of EMDR therapy as they are reprocessing trauma. The very object is a reminder of holding your ground. Using essential oils, scented candles, or other smellements can serve a similar purpose. You can also use spray bottles holding a mixture of water and several essential oil blends. Keep several of them around your office. Clients, after doing a gentle spray away from their body to test the scent, will have them available in your office to access both the textural element of feeling the water and the olfactory element of noticing the scent. In the Preparation phase, use of these multi-sensory elements can all be strengthened with slow bilateral stimulation/dual attention stimulus and then accessed when needed throughout the EMDR therapy.

Another skill for sensory grounding is walking meditation, with a focus on the sensation of the feet hitting the floor. Even in a small office, all that is needed is a four- to eight-foot walking path. Depending on the level of grounding needed, one can slow the walking to the level of super slow motion (like Jim Carrey in one of his films), and add verbal cues, either guided or self-guided. These might include "lifting," "stepping," "forward," "placing," and "grounding," or verbiage that further deepens the client's experience. For clients who are anchored and inspired by more poetic imagery, Thich Nhat Hahn's guided cue, "as I walk, my feet are kissing the earth," is lovely. The bilateral stimulation inherent in the act of walking also may help the client achieve a grounded state.

Listening to sound, whether nature sounds or music of the client's choosing, is another option. Consider having your client make a personal playlist of particularly healing music in a genre or combination of genres. During Preparation you can experiment with strengthening these with bilateral stimulation; after the session, the client will have the music to access. Taste might be used in a similar way: Something as simple as strengthening the sensation and taste of one's favorite tea as it moves through the body could be a valuable resource, as could the sensation of hot or cool water. In several of his autobiographical writings, the Dalai Lama (1990) shares that when he was a young man he drank large amounts of a Tibetan classic called butter tea. He eventually realized that his body was craving the warmth rather than the taste of the tea, so he switched to primarily consuming hot water as a stress reducer. In many of his works, he recommends drinking hot water and really connecting to the warming sensation.

Guided Visualizations

As you examine the following scripts for three visualization skills, consider where there may be room for improvisation and creativity in working with clients who may struggle with traditional visualization. This collection is by no means exhaustive. You can always encourage your EMDR clients or consultees to bring forward ideas for visualizations that they read in other resources, EMDR-specific or not. These exercises can be used as general visualizations. You can use the bullet points as guideposts for where you can apply the slow, bilateral stimulation/dual attention stimulus if the responses you are getting are adaptive.

LIGHT STREAM MULTISENSORY VISUALIZATION EXERCISE

- Imagine that a bright and healing light has begun to form overhead. This light can be whatever color you want it to be, whatever you associate with healing, happiness, goodness, or any other positive quality. If you don't like the idea of a light, you can think of it simply as a color or an essence. What are you noticing?

- Now, think about this light beginning to move through your body or over your body like a shield or force field (your choice), from the top of your head, moving inch by inch, slowly, until it reaches the bottom of your feet. What are you noticing now?

- Spend a few moments just hanging out with the presence of this light or essence in your body. Notice if it has any other qualities besides color, like a texture or a sound or a smell. What are you noticing now?

- Draw your attention back to where you first may have cued your body stress. What's happened to it? If the distress is still there on some level in your body, think about deepening your belly breathing so it makes the light or essence more brilliant and intense, so brilliant and intense that the distress can't even dream of existing within it.

- Keep practicing the exercise, in the attitude of patience, if you don't notice much of a shift the first time. If you have a spiritual practice and feel comfortable bringing in one of your spiritual or religious principles into the exercise, you are welcome to do that.

TREE GROUNDING VISUALIZATION EXERCISE

- Whether you are sitting or standing, notice the connection of your feet to the ground below you. Take a few moments here. Maybe pump your feet back and forth a few times and then let them come to stillness. Really be mindful of the connection.

- If this works for you, imagine that roots are coming out of your feet and shooting into the earth below you, like the roots of a tree.

- Notice the roots moving deep, deep, deep into the earth, through all of the different layers. Take a moment to just be with this experience. Think of yourself being firmly rooted in the earth, in the here and now.

MODIFICATIONS FOR CREATIVITY

- For children or willing adults, have them name what kind of tree they are (e.g., an oak, a banyan, an elm, a pine, etc.).

- If you have earth elements around your office, such as essential oils like cedar wood or pine, or even a Mason jar full of dirt (try it, it smells like the "good earth"), consider bringing those in—it can add to the grounding experience.

SIMPLE CONTAINER VISUALIZATION EXERCISE

- In this exercise, we will help you choose a visual that you can use to "pack away" memories, emotions, body sensations, or anything else that you are not quite ready to deal with, or that we may not have time to address in a specific session.

- Containers come in various shapes, and they can hold things for us that we are not quite ready to digest and address. What are some examples of containers that you can think of? A Mason jar? A shelf with a drawer? A piece of Tupperware? A tin? A backpack? Pick a visual representation of a container that works for you. Although many containers may work for this purpose, try to pick something that has great meaning or significance to you. What are you coming up with?

- Picture yourself opening the container. Send in or picture yourself placing whatever you may need to place in the container. Consider that this exercise is not about stuffing it away. It's simply helping you to manage the negativity until you are ready to deal with it. What are you noticing now?

- Close the container. Notice the experience and any sensations that come up with closing the container. Remember to breath evenly. What are you noticing now?

- If you wish, you can give your container a name or a phrase. You can use this to remind you of the container if you are feeling distressed.

Movement, Expressive Arts, and Identification of Other Recovery Capital

For clients who thrive on creativity, you can bolster the possibilities in Phase 2. The container exercise, a classic used by many EMDR trainers, offers numerous possibilities. Many clients prefer to make a container or bring in a vessel of some type to optimally resonate with the exercise. Clients have brought in backpacks that they've chosen to decorate and have with them as a physical symbol. Using a container like a shoebox or a plain jewelry box (available at many craft stores) allows for decorating with markers, paint, and other collage elements that can be affixed with glue. Richard, a former EMDR client, decorated a coffee tin for use as a container. He brought it to sessions as a visual symbol. Between sessions, he would write what was bothering him on slips of paper and put it in the coffee can. Many clients in addiction recovery are accustomed to using a similar technique called a "God box," with the box or the vessel being symbolic of a spiritual figure receiving what you are turning over.

Challenge your clients to explore outside of your office as part of their healing journey. Reconnecting or delving deeper into their hobbies and interests, or enrolling beloved pets as allies in the healing process are all viable methods for bottom up healing to take place. Many clients choose to receive bodywork or energy modalities like reiki as an adjunct to their psychotherapy. Great success can ensure when clients have connected with competent and trauma-sensitive providers. For many clients, seeking out or deepening connection with a faith community or church can also be helpful, although as clinicians take care to assess whether or not engagement with certain groups could potentially be replicating prior trauma dynamics. As clinicians we generally encourage exploration with resources and recovery capital, yet it is important to help clients evaluate whether these resources have more adaptive or maladaptive qualities.

Work with your client to develop a plan for how these resources can best be accessed. Addiction counselors have done this for years, recommending 12-step meetings in the community to clients. In this day and age, those recommendations are still relevant, and newer styles of fellowships such as Buddhist-based *Refuge Recovery* meetings are continuing to grow. Related to mindfulness and the holistic arts, perhaps you do some online searching with your clients, or suggest that they do some of their own research about meditation groups and classes now offered in many communities. Blue Star Family Counseling, a trauma-focused practice in Cortland, Ohio (where all clinicians are EMDR trained), offers a regular 8-week meditation class at a low cost. The same practice makes drop-in meditation groups and various styles of yoga available to their clients and to the larger community as well. Many in the Buddhist mindfulness and secular mindfulness community are finding their initial and ongoing teachings on podcasts, many, if not most, of which are free. For example, Against the Stream Buddhist Meditation Society posts many of the talks given at their Los Angeles and San Francisco centers, allowing students worldwide to take in talks and guided meditations for their use. Also, in addition to Buddhist centers, secular mindfulness centers set up in the tradition of yoga studios with drop-in classes are starting to pop up in many areas. Talks and guided meditations from a variety of teachers including Tara Brach, Jack Kornfield, Jon Kabat-Zinn, and others are freely available on YouTube and other distribution points.

Classes in yoga, tai chi, qigong, and other conscious dance or movement may also be viable options for your clients. Some basic movement practices appear in Chapter 4. If types of exercise resonate with clients, or if they struggle with them and you believe a well-guided class may help them to see the value of movement, consider making a suggestion. Not all classes are necessarily good fits for clients, so it may be advisable to get a sense of what classes and teachers are available in a community before recommending one to your client. Many teachers of these practices can have more of a fitness mindset and may not be well attuned to issues of trauma sensitivity. On the other side of this coin, more classes and workshops specifically geared for trauma-informed or recovery yoga are becoming available. If you are not sure of what's available in your community, consider asking around for referrals from colleagues or contacts who may engage in these types of classes. Encourage clients to check out at least three types of classes at three different places before they make a definitive judgment about whether movement classes are for them. If cost is an issue, many yoga studios in cities throughout the United States and Canada are known to offer periodic donation-based classes and workshops. A growing number of programs are seeking to make yoga and movement practices available to those who traditionally have not been able to access them. Please visit the resources list at the end of this chapter on some ideas for where you can start to search for these community resources in movement, wellness, meditation, and recovery.

TYING IT ALL TOGETHER

In some quarters, particularly during the early years of its genesis, EMDR therapy gained a reputation as a cold, clinical exercise. Many came to see it as a magic pill to bring out for quick resolution to what were unfortunately complex problems. Nothing could be further from the truth when EMDR therapy is presented as a complete approach and practiced as such. A mindful approach and mindful energy allows you to work on possibly the most important collaborative resourcing effort of all, the decision-making process as to whether the client is ready to move on to Phases 3 through 6, the dedicated reprocessing of traumatic memories. Having collaborated for a time in the realm of history, preparation, mindfulness training, and resourcing, clinicians can confidently move clients into the next phases of work. We may come back here again even in moving forward. The process is a dance to navigate: building resources, reprocessing, reassessing readiness. Clinicians can do what we need to do in the first two phases as thoroughly as possible. The fruits of Phase 2, Preparation do not disappear as we move forward. They remain as a strong foundation for the work ahead and a safe haven to return to whenever necessary.

QUESTIONS FOR REFLECTION AND PERSONAL PRACTICE

- How can the mindfulness practices I've learned thus far help me widen the possibilities of preparation in EMDR therapy?

- What factors, if any, keep me from thinking outside of the box with EMDR Phase 2, Preparation?

- What are my own fears and trepidations about moving clients from Phase 2 into Phase 3?

- How can developing a mindfulness practice (or strengthening an existing practice) help me to address these fears and trepidations?

RESOURCES FOR FURTHER EXPLORATION

Information on community-based classes and other resources that can be used to expand your practice can be found at:

- Against the Stream Buddhist Meditation Society: An international Buddhist meditation group founded by Noah Levine, with centers in Los Angeles and San Francisco and satellite groups around the country and internationally. Group meetings and other mindfulness resources including podcasts can be found on the website.
  www.againstthestream.org

- The Breathe Network: A national listing of providers in several modalities (e.g., bodywork, yoga, meditation, psychotherapy, intuitive healing, energy work) who identify as trauma-informed.
  www.thebreathenetwork.org

- Conscious Dancer Magazine: The official publication of the Dance-First Association, it provides links to events, classes, and communities within conscious and ecstatic dance.
  www.consciousdancer.com

- Dancing Mindfulness: The movement and expressive arts community founded by Dr. Jamie Marich provides links to dancing mindfulness communities, classes, and resources in the United States, Canada, and emerging areas globally.
  www.dancingmindfulness.com

- Exhale to Inhale: A nonprofit organization dedicated to promoting trauma-informed yoga training and advocacy; a listing of some free and low-cost classes and trainings are available on the website.
  www.exhaletoinhale.org

- InTheRooms.com: An inclusive directory of 12-step-based and alternative recovery programs includes a platform hosting several hundred web-based weekly meetings using video technology.
www.intherooms.com

- Refuge Recovery and Refuge Recovery Centers: A peer-led addiction recovery program based on the Four Noble Truths and the Eightfold Path of the Buddha. A list of meetings nationally and internationally, along with literature on how to start and conduct meetings, is available on the website.
www.refugerecovery.org

- Street Yoga: A nonprofit organization founded by Mark Lilly that aims to train facilitators to carry yoga into underprivileged communities. Select classes specific to Street Yoga are available in the Pacific Northwest; trainings are offered nationally.
www.streetyoga.com

- Yoga of 12-Step Recovery: A modality founded by Nikki Myers that combines a general 12-step meeting format and a yoga class for working with somatic elements of recovery. Meeting communities are available globally.
www.y12sr.com

- Yoga Unchained: The trauma-informed yoga training program co-founded by Dr. Jamie Marich and Jessica Sowers is offered as a component of a larger expressive arts therapy training program.
www.yogaunchained.com

- Yoganonymous: It provides a comprehensive list of yoga classes and studios across the United States and Canada.
www.yoganonymous.com

REFERENCES

Cloitre, M., Courtois, C. A., Ford, J. D., Green, B. L., Alexander, P., Briere, J., . . . van der Hart, O. (2012). *The ISTSS expert consensus treatment guidelines for complex PTSD in adults.* Retrieved from http://www.istss.org/AM/Template.cfm?Section=ISTSS _Complex_PTSD_Treatment_Guidelines&Template=/CM/ContentDisplay .cfm&ContentID=5185

Dalai Lama. (1990). *Freedom in exile: The autobiography of the Dalai Lama.* New York, NY: HarperCollins.

De Jongh, A., Resick, P. A., Zoellner, L. A., Van Minnen, A., Lee, C. W., Monson, C. M., . . . Bicanic, I. A. (2016). Critical analysis of the current treatment guidelines for complex PTSD in adults. *Depression and Anxiety, 33,* 359–369. doi:10.1002/da.22469

Duncan, B. L., Miller, S. D., Wampold, B. E., & Hubble, M. A. (Eds.). (2009). *The heart and soul of change: Delivering what works in therapy* (2nd ed.). Washington, DC: American Psychological Association.

Dworkin, M. (2005). *EMDR and the relational imperative: The therapeutic relationship in EMDR treatment.* New York, NY: Brunner-Routledge.

Dworkin, M., & Errebo, N. (2010). Rupture and repair in the EMDR client/clinician relationship: Now moments and moments of meeting. *Journal of EMDR Practice and Research, 4*(3), 113–123.

EMDR International Association. (2012). *EMDRIA definition of EMDR.* Austin, TX: Author. Retrieved from http://c.ymcdn.com/sites/www.emdria.org/resource/resmgr/Definition/EMDRIADefinitionofEMDR.pdf

Korn, D., & Leeds, A. (2002). Preliminary evidence of efficacy for EMDR resource development and installation in the stabilization phase of treatment of complex posttraumatic stress disorder. *Journal of Clinical Psychology, 58,* 1465–1487.

Leeds, A. (2016). *A guide to the standard EMDR therapy protocols for clinicians, supervisors and consultants* (2nd ed.). New York, NY: Springer Publishing.

MacLean, P. D. (1990). *The triune brain in evolution: Role in paleocerebral functions.* New York, NY: Plenum Press.

Manfield, P. (2003). *EMDR casebook: Expanded second edition.* New York, NY: W. W. Norton.

Marich, J. (2010). EMDR in addiction continuing care: A phenomenological study of women in early recovery. *Psychology of Addictive Behaviors, 24*(3), 498–507.

Marich, J. (2012). What makes a good EMDR therapist? Exploratory clients from client-centered inquiry. *Journal of Humanistic Psychology, 52*(4), 401–422.

Parnell, L. (2007). *A therapist's guide to EMDR: Tools and techniques for successful treatment.* New York, NY: W. W. Norton.

Parnell, L. (2013). *Attachment-focused EMDR: Healing relational trauma.* New York, NY: W. W. Norton.

Shapiro, F. (2001). *Eye movement desensitization and reprocessing: Basic principles, protocols, and procedures* (2nd ed.). New York, NY: Guilford Press.

Sonoma Psychotherapy Training Institute. (2012). *What is EMDR?* Video series with Dr. Andrew Leeds and Dr. Stephen Dansiger. Retrieved from https://www.youtube.com/playlist?list=PLoB6Y5vULDT4bKPXvsFR13aqQt_GTGTUC

Van der Kolk, B. (2014). *The body keeps the score: Brain, mind, and body in the healing of trauma.* New York, NY: Viking.

7

EMDR Phases 3 to 6: Principles of Mindful Decision Making

MOVING ON TO PHASES 3 TO 6

In the next two chapters, Phases 3 to 6 are covered as one unit, referred to as the reprocessing phases of EMDR (Eye Movement Desensitization and Reprocessing) therapy. For many people in the public arena who have seen only video demonstration clips of EMDR therapy or an article touting the accelerated effects of EMDR therapy, Phases 3 to 6 are the crux of EMDR therapy. Shapiro designed the method, the technology, for transforming how traumatic memories are stored in the brain with Phases 3 to 6. These phases—some of which can move quickly and others, particularly Phase 4, slowly—constitute the heart of the EMDR approach to psychotherapy.

In this chapter, the lens of mindfulness and mindfulness-based decision making is employed to help you approach these reprocessing phases with greater ease and clarity. This process starts by examining the factors that the clinician must consider before moving into Phases 3 to 6 from Phase 2, Preparation. Once you and your client have collaboratively decided to move into Phases 3 to 6, you will be asked to consider that there are many elements of mindfulness in what we collectively refer to as Shapiro's standard setup and targeting sequence. You will discover how teaching mindfulness in the Preparation phase, even in small increments, facilitates your success in Phases 3 to 6.

CLINICAL DECISION-MAKING POINTS

The decision about whether a client is adequately prepared to move from Phase 2 into Phase 3 is one that must be made on a case-by-case basis. As noted throughout the book, one Calm Safe Place exercise is rarely sufficient. So what is sufficient? Because of the intricacies of the human experience, you cannot use a simple checklist or an easy flow chart. It is inevitable that for every rule there is at least one exception, and in the case of complex trauma and dissociation there are often more exceptions than rules. You may, however, benefit from using these questions to guide your clinical decision making. These questions are not to be approached like a checklist or test. Although it may be tempting to declare, "Well, the answer is *yes* to five of these questions, so let's move along," that is not the intent of these questions. The hope is that these questions will guide you in building your clinical intuition as an EMDR therapist. If you are working with a consultant at this stage of your EMDR training journey, these questions may serve as a useful aid in the consultation process.

The decision about moving into Phases 3 to 6 is ultimately collaborative; both client and clinician must participate in the process. Mindfully evaluating each of these areas, with direct feedback from the client if appropriate, will help you to fill in any gaps in preparation that may need to be addressed before moving into the trauma reprocessing phases. Revisiting these questions can also be valuable if you begin Phases 3 to 6 with a client and they balk or otherwise state that the EMDR is too much for them. In Exhibit 7.1, you will see a quick reference to the clinical decision-making questions. Clinical commentary on each question follows.

EXHIBIT 7.1 Quick Reference Table: Clinical Decision Making in Transitioning to Phase 3

> - *Does the client have a reasonable amount of preparation skills to access?*
> - *Is there a sufficient amount of positive material in the client's life?*
> - *What is the nature of the living situation?*
> - *Have you looked at the picture with psychotropic medication and other drug or alcohol use?*
> - *Have you assessed for secondary gains and other related issues?*
> - *Have you considered the number of sessions available?*
> - *Is the client willing (and ready) to look at past issues? Can targets be adjusted accordingly if they are not?*

Access to Preparation Skills

EMDR therapists have their favorite words, phrases, and ideas in addressing this issue. Whether you call them coping skills, self-soothing skills, distress tolerance skills, balancing techniques, affect regulation mechanisms, mindfulness approaches, resource development methods, or simply resources, it is key that the client has a series of them that they are working to apply in daily life. First, recognize that there are a variety of names and models to implement this general idea, and perhaps involve the client in determining which phrase or conceptual description works best for them. Some clients resonate with the idea of "resourcing"; others may prefer "coping skills" or "distress tolerance." Use what will stick for them. Take, for instance, Luke, a client presenting for services who met the criteria for mild mental retardation. A recovering alcoholic with a history of developmental trauma, Luke embraced the treatment process with enthusiasm. He described his early learning in treatment as "the things I do so I don't recollapse." His own word *recollapse*, as opposed to the traditional word *relapse*, resonated so effectively for him that his therapist did not even dream of correcting him.

After working with a client like Luke to build a set of skills (options and strategies covered in the previous chapter), it is vital to determine if the client is using the skills outside of session. Indeed, some clients may come for services already well prepared and are used to working with a variety of coping strategies. While accounting for use outside of session may not take on the same sense of urgency with such clients, it is still important to evaluate how all your clients are able to use the skills when they need them in life. For instance, a yoga teacher may present for services and articulate fantastic conceptual understanding of all the major breath techniques. The teacher may even be able to teach you a thing or two about how to adjust your teaching of these breath practices, having had long experience with students. However, if the client reports or expresses an inability to access the breath to cope with stress or ride out difficult emotion in daily life, there is still a gap that needs to be addressed. What is keeping such a client from actually using the breath practices, and how can we suggest a plan of action? These are the types of questions mindful EMDR therapists will learn to ask and evaluate in their practice.

The issue of implementing skills in between sessions generally takes on greater importance with clients who have had little or no exposure to healthy or adaptive methods of coping, or with cases of complex trauma and dissociation. The reality is that even though EMDR therapy has been touted as a more accelerated way to target traumatic memories that does not necessitate clients diving into the details of traumatic narrative, EMDR Phases 3 through 6 can elicit emotional intensity, unexpected body sensations, and unpredictable shifts in affect. Can the client in question handle those shifts? Many standard training approaches talk a great deal about orienting a client to these possibilities. A mindful approach to EMDR therapy accepts this general orientation and takes it a step further—what do the client and clinician need to do, collaboratively, to get the client ready for this process? Too many clients will respond to EMDR orientation with some version of "I can't handle this." A mindful response challenges, "What do we need to do to get you prepared to handle that which you fear, especially if your goal is to work through the impact of this traumatic experience on your life?"

A few final notes on implementation: Clients are generally good about telling on themselves when you check in about use of the skills in daily life. Consider those clients who are excited to tell you about how a skill that you covered in session worked for them when they were in the middle of a stressful experience. Contrast that with clients who, when you asked them if they practiced the breath technique you worked on last session, said that they forgot. It is vital to respond as compassionately and as nonjudgmentally as possible, and then go on to develop some suggestions and, hopefully, a plan for how they can be reminded to use these skills in daily life. More suggestions for those strategies appear in Chapter 6.

Positive Material in the Client's Life

Many EMDR therapists wait too long before moving into Phases 3 to 6 with clients because they are waiting for them to become "more stable" or for life to get "a little less crazy." Professionals working in the addiction field can be particularly nervous about timing. Many clinicians operate from a place of near-paranoia about treatments that process trauma, making clients worse. However, many clients may not be able to achieve a sense of enhanced stability in life until they have addressed some of their traumatic triggers, a position that is now supported by research relating to complex posttraumatic stress disorder (PTSD) clients (De Jongh et al., 2016).

This timing and stability issue, like many on this list, cannot be addressed with black-and-white answers. It is naive to assume that just because EMDR is not as narratively focused as other trauma therapies, it does not come with some potential for intensity. While life does not have to be anywhere near perfect or even ideal to flow into EMDR Phases 3 through 6, it is at least wise to evaluate some of the positives that exist in a client's life. Do they have friends, healthy family members, or other recovery contacts who know that they are in therapy? Are they able to share with such friends that this new therapy they will be trying, EMDR therapy, may involve some emotionally charged sessions requiring some self-care afterward? Might these individuals be available for a phone call to offer support in between sessions? These are just some examples of skills you might build in preparation (e.g., accessing support) that must be evaluated at this juncture.

For clients who are heavily isolated, these questions may seem like a luxury. As the clinician, have you considered linking them to other sources of community support, such as case management or self-help/mutual help meetings and groups in the community? The absence of positive material in a client's life does not rule out moving into Phases 3 through 6 of EMDR therapy, although it may require that you work toward helping them build some, even if this includes engaging in practices such as resource development and installation (RDI). Consider Luisa, a client with complex developmental trauma, who appeared to have few healthy people accessible in her life for support. However, the client had a very close connection to her two pets. After each therapy session, her ritual was to go back to her apartment and play with her pets, telling them about how her therapy session went. This ritual and mammalian connection, along with some other distress tolerance skills done in preparation, helped both Luisa and her EMDR therapist feel comfortable about proceeding.

Nature of the Living Situation

These questions are not about looking for some ideal state of being to come into existence before moving into Phases 3 through 6. This theme recurs throughout the set of questions and especially rings true in examining the living situation It is probably unrealistic to expect that all our clients will be able to live in a situation where they experience ideal safety and support 24 hours a day, 7 days a week. A better question may be how to help clients create a greater sense of safety for themselves if changing their living situation is not practical or feasible.

EMDR therapy consultants often field a variety of questions around living situations. What about kids who are living with emotionally abusive parents? What about prison inmates, who, although they may have access to treatment, may not feel safe? What about individuals in addiction recovery living in a house where others use drugs and alcohol? Many EMDR clinicians opt to err on the side of caution and not proceed to Phases 3 to 6 in these and in similar situations, preferring instead to focus on resourcing or preparation-level skills and supportive counseling. Many EMDR therapists have discovered that if a client is as prepared as possible and able to access other viable resources you have cultivated in Phase 2, proceeding is possible. In situations where you, as the clinician, are not optimally comfortable with the living situation (particularly when the client is unsure as well), it may be wise not to begin targeting with the earliest, touchstone memory. Rather, start with targeting the living situation itself or another target that may ultimately prove to be a gentler way to begin Phases 3 to 6. More detail on this strategy appears in the final question of this section.

Drug/Alcohol Use and Psychotropic Medication

Shapiro and other EMDR therapy leaders have long advised that EMDR can be practiced with clients who are on psychotropic medications, provided they are stable on their medications. Thus, it would not be wise to begin Phases 3 to 6 when a client is undergoing a medication change; evaluate a few weeks of stability and positive response with a medication change, consulting with the prescriber if possible. Shapiro's original recommendation (2001) about clients deciding to wean off psychotropic medications is also sound. If a client has been on a psychotropic medication and, with the guidance of his or her prescriber, decides to discontinue the pharmacotherapy or make a major change, emphasis on Phase 8, Reevaluation, is warranted. Determine if any residual disturbances that surface after the change of course in medical treatment may be appropriate to address with additional preparation skills and targeting (Phases 3–6 work).

The two classifications of psychotropic medications that have highlighted themselves as potentially problematic to the flow of EMDR therapy are benzodiazepines and alpha- and beta-blockers, often prescribed for residual anxiety, nightmares, and other nonpsychiatric conditions such as heart problems. Benzodiazepines have caught the attention of many EMDR therapists. Although pharmacological treatment guidelines for PTSD from organizations such as the Food and Drug Administration and the World Health Organization do not approve of or discourage their use, many prescribers resort to benzodiazepines to treat presenting symptoms such as panic and sleep disturbances. Many EMDR therapists who are also addiction specialists become concerned when this phenomenon shows potential for dependence. Even if dependence was not a risk, there is still an issue at play as it relates to EMDR therapy Phases 3 through 6—benzodiazepines work neurologically as a central nervous system depressant. For many survivors of trauma, these medications depress or suppress many of the problematic symptoms that manifest from their unhealed traumatic experiences. However, the same medications can also suppress what we are attempting to activate with Phases 3 to 6 of the EMDR protocol.

The same issue of central nervous system suppression also surfaces in considering other drugs—marijuana (even if medically prescribed), alcohol, and opioid pain medication. Thus, it may also be difficult for a client who is prescribed medical marijuana or receiving opioid pain management to have the fullest possible experience with the effects of EMDR therapy. This segues to another topic of debate in EMDR therapy circles: Can EMDR therapy, especially Phases 3 to 6, be performed on someone who is actively on these medications, whether obtained through medical channels or illicitly? What about a client who is actively drinking? In keeping with the theme of this section, it truly depends on a variety of variables.

For clients where addiction or dependence has been identified, examine where the client is at in the stages of change. A commonly used concept in the addiction field, developed by Prochaska and DiClemente (1982), the stages—precontemplation to change, contemplation, preparation, action, maintenance, and termination—are designed as a guide to determine what types of interventions we use with each client. For instance, it is unwise to suggest a plethora of action-based interventions (e.g., go to 90 AA meetings in 90 days, engage in intensive EMDR psychotherapy) with someone who is not even sure if they want to change. As explored in *EMDR Made Simple* (Marich, 2011) and *Treating Addictions With EMDR Therapy and the Stages of Change* (Abel & O'Brien, 2014), abstinence may not be the most important factor to address in moving to Phases 3 to 6. Rather, determining whether someone is in an action stage of change may prove more relevant. If they are not in an action stage of change, could EMDR Phase 2, Preparation, be used to help bring them to at least a preparation stage of change? Another possibility is to employ recovery-focused targeting sequences for initial engagement with Phases 3 to 6. Developing targeting sequences that address barriers to change is possible. For instance, floating back a core identity statement, such as "I'm not capable of change," may be a wiser way to begin Phases 3 to 6 work than going for the proverbial jugular with the earliest touchstone memory.

Use of specialty addiction protocols such as DeTUR (Desensitization of Triggers and Urge Reprocessing; Popky, 2005), CraveEx (Craving Extinguished; Hase, 2009), and the Feeling State Addiction Protocol (Miller, 2012) has been proposed as a gentler and more relevant way to begin reprocessing work with individuals who are still using any of the chemicals we have mentioned in this section (Markus and Hornsveld, 2017). Although research on these approaches is limited, emerging inquiry (Wise & Marich, 2016) suggests that for EMDR clinicians who are already knowledgeable and skilled at working with addiction and compulsion, navigating between these specialty protocols and the standard protocol is possible, even with individuals who are not totally abstinent. In working with addiction and compulsion, it is important for EMDR therapists to have a modicum of understanding about the dynamics of addiction and compulsion and not view EMDR therapy as the "quick fix." Intricacies in decision making are needed, and here is another place where taking the mindful view is helpful. Seek consultation about addiction from another EMDR therapist who specializes in it or knows it well if you are stuck.

Collaborating and consulting with prescribers after obtaining a necessary release may also be helpful. If your clinical assessment is that addiction or compulsive use is an issue, or if the medication a person is taking may be hindering EMDR Phases 3 to 6 from working optimally, such consultation may be compulsory. Although nonprescribing clinicians have to be very careful not to work outside of our scope of practice, we often have to address the possibility of medication interference with clients and encourage them to advocate for themselves to prescribers. A particularly frustrating type of client is the person who presents for services after having read a miracle story online about EMDR therapy working in 2 to 3 sessions. Although addressing expectations is often required as a general best practice, this task takes on more significant implications if a person is on a variety of central nervous system depressants such as benzodiazepines, opioid pain medication, or medical marijuana. In such circumstances, if a person is not willing to talk to their prescribers about dosing or looking at alternative methods for relief, a useful strategy is to explain: "We can certainly give EMDR therapy a try; however, you are encouraged to keep your expectations realistic about how quickly the EMDR will work. We may have to use trial and error and make several adjustments to how we do the EMDR therapy after seeing if the medication may or may not interfere with your response."

Talking to the prescriber about time of day for dosing can be helpful. In the experience of many EMDR therapists, clients who present for EMDR Phases 3 to 6 without having taken their benzodiazepine dose yet that day or who have not smoked marijuana that day are able to achieve some movement in trauma reprocessing. Although alpha- and beta-blockers are generally not seen as abusable or addictive, they can keep EMDR therapy from working to its fullest potential. Thus, having a similar conversation with a prescriber or encouraging the client to have such a conversation with a prescriber about dosing is also warranted. This specific area of inquiry might interest a client who is determined to engage in EMDR therapy and seems to be working very hard at it, yet not noticing much of an effect.

Secondary Gains and Related Issues

It is impossible to do trauma work without considering the impact of secondary gains. The potential benefits of staying stuck or not treating one's disorder or diagnosis can vary. The tangible advantages, such as disability benefits or access to certain prescriptions (e.g., benzodiazepines, medical marijuana), tend to generate the most attention. However, other benefits, such as having an excuse when challenged about behaviors (e.g., "I act like this because I'm crazy from what happened to me!") or shaping one's identity around the traumatic experience, are also possible and present even more of an interference.

The presence of secondary gains does not rule out taking a client into Phases 3 through 6 of EMDR therapy. However, within the context of an established therapeutic relationship, it can be important to have a discussion with your client about how life may change before you proceed with Phase 3. Sometimes, this conversation organically happens after you attempt the reprocessing phases of EMDR therapy where minimal movement is witnessed. There are a variety of reasons that people may "resist" the process working for them. "Resist" appears within quotation marks because it is a concept clinicians commonly reference, yet a trauma-focused approach suggests that all resistance originates somewhere. People may cite a variety of reasons for not allowing themselves to process or move toward their goals. Fear of change is commonly mentioned, yet for many clients it is the fear of economic insecurity that presents itself when one thinks about changing. Many clients express fear about leaving an unhealthy yet financially secure relationship or employment situation as a major factor in choosing not to make the changes that they need to make. Some clients explain that they fear losing connection to you as their therapist should they get better. This gain might be especially significant if you are the first person who has ever shown them any kind of respect or validation.

The solutions here are various and must be navigated on the basis of client and context. Sometimes, a simple conversation, either before you have moved to Phase 3 or after you have attempted Phases 3 to 6 and not witnessed much effect, does the trick. If you and the client are particularly ambitious, consider how the gain itself may contain a negative cognition (e.g., "I cannot make it on my own," "I will fail if I try something new," "My trauma experience is my identity") that can be floated back to arrive at some earlier memory. Whatever gets unearthed after asking the floatback can potentially be set up as a new targeting sequence.

Number of Sessions Available

The importance of evaluating this question in our decision making is to determine whether we have enough time with the client to ethically cover what the client revealed during Phase 1, Client History. Insurance or other third-party payers sometimes restrict how many sessions a client can access. Even private-pay clients may be taken by surprise if they've read online that EMDR therapy is not going to take very long. They may discover that funds are limited and grow frustrated when it seems that EMDR work is going to take longer than originally anticipated. As mentioned in the EMDRIA definition of EMDR, it is important to explain to clients that EMDR does not happen in any set number of sessions. One way of saying this is found in a slogan in the 12-step tradition: "More will be revealed." Although the intention of sharing a similar sentiment with EMDR clients is not to suggest that they will be in therapy the rest of their lives (on the contrary), it may assist clinicians in helping them to keep expectations realistic.

Having an unlimited number of sessions for work is not necessarily the opposite ideal. Many EMDR therapists see clients with either unlimited benefits or unlimited ability to pay. Such clients may stall in their work, insisting "We have all the time in the world to get to that EMDR" or "We'll do it next week." Some of the greatest successes in EMDR therapy observed clinically are when people have a deadline, for instance: "I want to address this issue before I start my new job" or "It's important to me to work through this before my child is born." Even with clients without specific deadlines, the same spirit of helping people identify a clear, measurable goal can help with the overall conceptualization and flow. For more on this, please visit our sample treatment plan in Chapter 5.

Willingness to Examine Past Issues and Potential Target Adjustments

Shapiro teaches that to obtain the optimal generalization effect and treatment impact of EMDR therapy, clinicians must help clients identify the first and/or the worst memory related to their presenting issue. Shapiro (2001) cautions in her text that in complex cases going back to the touchstone memory may not be the ideal. The EMDRIA definition of EMDR Therapy, operating from the spirit of Shapiro's three-pronged protocol, indicates that the order in which the three prongs—past, present, and future—are processed can be modified on the basis of clinical judgement. EMDR therapists who work primarily with complex trauma clients and clients with addictive and compulsive disorders have likely realized that these "exceptional" cases are more likely to manifest as the rule, or the norm. The reality with such cases is that going back to the earliest and/or the worst memory can be too overwhelming, even with a well-executed preparation phase.

When a client expresses a reluctance to go back to the past just yet, that does not rule out moving forward with Phase 3. It means that you may have to make some modifications to the textbook operating procedure. In doing so, many clinicians fear that they are deviating from the standard protocol that they were taught in training. However, thinking outside the box about target sequence planning as you move a client into Phase 3 may be essential for safety. If you respect the overall treatment plan, any resistance that may have surfaced during Phases 1 and 2 and the permission given to you through the EMDRIA definition of EMDR to adjust the order of the prongs based on clinical judgment will still leave you in good shape.

As an example, let us look at a common response from many clients when the treatment transitions into Phase 3: "I don't think I can handle looking at my past." Phase 1, Client History may have revealed a multitude of traumas, many of them in early development, that need to be processed for optimal treatment effect. Yet if the client is stuck from even going there (or if a client in recovery is concerned about relapse if they get too emotionally overwhelmed by going to the past), why not use the negative cognition underlying that sentiment to set up a targeting sequence? Perhaps floating back "I can't handle it" will reveal an earlier attempt at recovery where clients believe that they failed. Thus, we are using the present prong (the most significant presenting issue of being stuck or blocked) to do a floatback to a past event. Although it may not be as far back as clients will eventually need to go to meet their goals, targeting in this manner respects the spirit of starting somewhere charged, ushering in the process of allowing the brain to go where it needs to go. Targeting in this fashion can be the proverbial gentler path that people need to begin looking at their past, all the while giving them a more solid orientation to EMDR in the process. This strategy is one of our many ounces of prevention that can be worth a pound of cure when it comes to keeping complex clients engaged in EMDR therapy.

FACILITATING A CLIENT'S JOURNEY THROUGH PHASES 3 TO 6

MINDFULNESS IN PHASES 3 TO 6

Providers of EMDR therapy trainings following the guidelines of an organization such as EMDRIA or its national organization teach Phases 3 through 7 as something Shapiro referred to as the 11-step targeting sequence. In this section, the eleventh step is omitted because it is about closure and is handled in its own chapter to follow. Although specific language nuances may vary among providers, this 11-step protocol is well known by those trained in EMDR therapy. For reference, the steps and their corresponding phases or questions are listed. These steps are followed by an explanation of how much mindfulness philosophy and strategies indicative of mindfulness meditation are inherent in what is commonly called "the protocol." By contemplating this inherence, you can experience greater confidence about carrying the fruits of your personal mindfulness practice and study into navigating the tricky situations that may arise in Phases 3 to 6.

Phase 3: Assessment

▶ **Image or worst part:** *Looking back on it now, what image represents the worst part of the target? (NOTE: If no image is available or image does not carry much charge, simply have client use another sensory channel, such as sound, or think about the target.)*

Mindfulness practice begins right here at the first step of the protocol. In one fell swoop, clinicians direct the client toward *this* moment ("Looking back on it *now*") while simultaneously evoking the past. The casual observer or client new to this process may think this step a torturous exercise when, in fact, clinicians are opening a door through which a client can move quickly, a door to reprocessing. Earlier work done by the client during the resourcing phase, including such visualizations as the Light Stream, may help them to locate an image that is the preferred sense memory, as it tends to be most evocative of itself as well as other sensory channels. The classical mindfulness skill of simply noticing present moment experiences with as little judgment as possible helps tether the client to the direct experience of how the memory is affecting them in their life today, as opposed to what the experience was like in the past. This is critical for successful reprocessing. The client and therapist with mindfulness training will be more likely to accomplish this task. A therapist fully engaged in the moment can help orient a client into that same present moment. A client with mindfulness training can sit with discomfort long enough to identify the source, the manifestations, and the depth of the suffering, while making connections to the experience of this very moment.

▶ **Negative cognition (NC):** *When you bring up that image or worst part now, what is the negative belief about yourself that goes along with it?*

Here, the process involves another level of mindfulness. With the image and worst part, clients access the story created and stored in the mind. That story is incomplete and inaccurate, the result of maladaptive processing. By placing mindful attention upon it, adaptive reprocessing can begin by looking at the story anew and placing it in the light of awareness. With Negative Cognition, the process journeys a little deeper into the maladaptively created storyline. Clinicians guide clients into the deep end of the pool, in a Buddhist mindfulness sense. The first step in the target setup reflects the third foundation of mindfulness, Mindfulness of Mind, or thoughts and thought patterns. This second step goes into the last foundation of mindfulness, Mindfulness of Dharmas, or the mindfulness of more conceptual thought.

▶ **Positive cognition (PC):** *When you think of the image or worst part of the target, what would you like to believe about yourself now?*

Some clinicians, writers, and practitioners have opposed this step in the target setup as unnecessary (Marich, 2011; Parnell, 2007). Although many clients can struggle to come up with a positive cognition in Phase 3, it is important to at least ask and initially explore. This inquiry is another mindfulness exercise, as clients are encouraged to toggle from the negative material into the positive belief. If therapists do not mindfully lead the client to the positive belief as it specifically pertains to the traumatic memory elicited, the client may have a false sense of the level of positive belief based on their current overall well-being. "I am enough" may be a positive belief that the client is able to maintain in general when not triggered by difficult material or experiences. For clinicians, a goal here is to use our own mindfulness in consort with the client's mindfulness to focus in on the desired positive belief while holding the traumatic image. This serves the purpose of further activating the negative elements of the memory by perhaps showing the client how far away the positive remains, which is part of the maladaptive processing of the material. The recognition of the devastation on positive affect that the material has produced becomes part of the reprocessing right here in Phase 3.

▶ **Validity of Cognition (VoC):** *What is your gut-level feeling of how true that positive belief is right now as you look back on the image or worst part (with 1 being completely false and 7 being completely true)?*

The positive belief brings mindfulness to the general, and possibly abstract, belief that one would like to carry with the reprocessed memory. The Validity of Cognition (VoC) turns our mindfulness toward the affect and cognitions related to that belief as it stands now with the traumatic material coursing through our system. The tracking of the VoC provides a mindful bridge to the next aspect of the emotions. The mindfulness-based nature of this question is inherent in how it is used as a bridge. Clinicians are not asking the client to land on this positive belief and its level of truth, but rather laying a bridge between the cognitive elements of the material and the emotional reactions. Then, clinician and client leave the positive behind for the rest of desensitization and reprocessing until it is time for installation. These two steps, more than the others, are swift and impermanent stages of reprocessing.

▶ **Emotion**: *What emotion(s) do you feel when you link the image or worst part with the negative belief of _____?*

Mindfulness of emotional states can be very difficult for traumatized clients. Avoidance of these emotions may be the most important skill in their lives up until now. If we have done a good job of creating a set of mindfulness skills in ourselves and in our clients, and proceeded with them in the earlier steps of setting up the target, we have created a safe, or safer, space for the client to experience these emotions. At this point, clients are deep in the experience, guided there mindfully and with great loving kindness by the clinician.

▶ **Subjective Units of Disturbance (SUDs):** *What is your level of disturbance as you bring up the image or worst part, the negative belief, and the emotions all together (with 0 being no disturbance or neutral, and 10 being the worst you can imagine)?*

Attempting to consolidate the entire experience into a general level of disturbance is the next point of order. With mindful intention, the process draws up the image or the worst part, the negative belief about the self that exists in this moment when it is up front, and the emotions that were created by the negative aspects and exacerbated by the brief recognition of the lack of the positive. If mindfulness has been maintained and the process has kept moving, reprocessing will have already begun. Mindfulness of the general sense of disturbance brings together awareness of all the cognitive and emotion-based material, in order that we might switch gears in a moment and put our attention back on the body.

▶ **Location of Body Sensation:** *What are you noticing in your body in this moment as you bring up the image or worst part, the negative belief, and the emotions all together?*

Our last mindful act in setting up the target in Phase 3 is to notice what is happening in the body. In Buddhist mindfulness, placing mindful attention on the body is the first foundation of mindfulness. Here, the Phase 3 method places it last, as the landing pad for all that has been activated during the target setup. Often, clients hold so much pain and trauma in the body. This holding generally exists without a sense of mindfulness. Through a series of mindful concentration steps, the client has accessed all the elements of the maladaptively processed memory together, resulting in body sensations related to them. The method draws mindful attention to pain and suffering that is already present, placing it into a manifestation where clients can desensitize and reprocess the memory into a new form. This new form may eventually lead to a life free from those aspects of the memory that are not useful, as they will fall away. All other aspects of the memory will be transformed. The client will be able to live a more adaptive life, thereby making this target setup the proverbial exercise in short-term pain for long-term gain. Human beings need mindfulness of the body to create a sense of peace in the body. Thus, the process lands here in the body before heading into reprocessing.

Phase 4: Desensitization

▶ **Desensitize:** *Bring up that body sensation together with the negative belief of _____ and the image or worst part of the memory, and just notice whatever you notice as I begin the stimulation. (Continuing with stimulation until SUDs of target image are 0 or as close as possible and VoC of positive cognition is 7. Be sure to check if a new, more relevant PC has developed instead of the original one.)*

"Just notice." These words are at the heart of mindfulness practice, and are at the heart of the Desensitization phase of EMDR therapy. The client with mindfulness skills developed during the first two phases and utilized during Phase 3 will now be in good shape to engage with desensitization and reprocessing. We now enter an ongoing acceptance of impermanence and use it to our advantage. Rather than engaging in deep concentration, you are combining the bilateral DAS (dual attention stimulus) with the ongoing movement of the mind, body, and spirit to lead the reprocessing wherever it naturally goes. In more complex cases as well as in general practice, you may see a need for more than one interweave or other type of intervention. For the most part, however, the client's brain is doing the work, and clinicians are staying out of the way as much as possible. We are only checking the SUDs as an interweave when we spot looping or the stoppage of reprocessing. After that, clinicians apply more direct intervention only when positive material appears consistently and the end of a target nears. Phase 4 most directly brings the very definition of mindfulness into play, "non-judgmental present time awareness" (Kabat-Zinn, 2011). If clients and clinicians have done their work together until this point, we will find that reprocessing will flow. If not, clinicians can use their own mindfulness practice to see what is necessary to unplug to get reprocessing moving again. The result can be the client's SUDs moving down to a zero. Now, we see their mindful attention has shifted and deepened.

Phase 5: Installation

▶ **Install:** *Place that positive belief of* _____ *together with the original image or worst part. (Continue with 1–2 sets of stimulation to install; continue applying stimulation if time allows and more adaptive networks are connecting.)*

The initial, mindful foray into the positive belief during Phase 3 makes the installation phase that much more powerful. Now, the positive belief is not only within reach, but it is palpable and available. It has perhaps shifted from the earlier version into something that fits that much more succinctly with the image as it is now after reprocessing. Applying mindfulness to the changes that have occurred continues the reprocessing. The client then uses their mindfulness practice to be able to place the new positive belief together with the new version of the image created by desensitization and reprocessing. This completes the reprocessing, bringing mindful attention to the new world that the client has created within, assisted by mindful facilitation.

Phase 6: Body Scan

▶ **Body Scan:** *Now that the positive belief has been installed, scan your body from head to toe: What are you noticing? (Apply at least one set of stimulations to a* *clear or neutral body scan, holding it together with PC. If residual disturbance is reported, continue with stimulation until the scan is a clear or neutral body scan. Then, use a set of stimulations to pair the clear scan with the PC).*

As with the setup of the target, the process ends with the body and the reptilian brain. Having reprocessed all elements of the memory in relation to the neocortical and limbic systems, clinicians check one last time those aspects that can remain beneath our conscious awareness, those of the body. Once you establish mindfulness of the body reactions and see that they are clear, you can be much more secure in the knowledge that reprocessing of the target is complete. Mindfulness of the body is often framed as the gateway in Buddhist mindfulness. It can even be the source of enlightenment, or the end of suffering (Goldstein, 2013). Here, you can witness that happen through the application of phases of EMDR therapy to a particular area of suffering, landing in a clear body scan, opening the door to ongoing transformative mindfulness. Shapiro's protocol and millennia-old wisdom combine to provide healing of the trauma-inflicted wounding.

The target has been completed.

TYING IT ALL TOGETHER

The reprocessing phases of EMDR therapy are those aspects of EMDR that are most recognizable to the general public, and even to many in the general trauma therapy community and beyond. Even so, the most obvious opportunities we have to engage mindfully are found in the first and second phases of the eight-phase protocol, particularly as part of the Phase 2 task of resourcing. However, once we are at the end of Phase 2 and ready to make decisions about whether to move on to reprocessing, the outcomes of our initial mindful work together inform our ability to bring mindfulness to the remainder of the therapy.

A mindful approach to the transition from Phase 2 into Phases 3 through 6 is often the key to successful reprocessing. Maintaining mindfulness through this clinical decision-making process makes us more patient in our run-up to the reprocessing phases, which many therapists may feel like rushing into in the hope of bringing quick relief to the client. Mindfulness at this stage provides compassionate care for ourselves and our clients by establishing a solid base from which to do the heavy lifting. Once in the reprocessing phases, our own mindfulness practice makes us more likely to be in the state of mind to follow Shapiro's admonition to "stay out of the way as much as possible," and the client trained in mindfulness will become more adept at maintaining the ability to "just notice" and "go with that." From that foundation, we are able to find almost infinite possibilities to apply mindfulness to all aspects of the target assessment, the whole of the desensitization process, the installation of the positive cognition, and the body scan. As we head into Phase 7, Closure, whether the target is complete or incomplete, we have provided the tools necessary for continued reprocessing while maintaining safety for our continued work together.

QUESTIONS FOR REFLECTION AND PERSONAL PRACTICE

- What are some of the most challenging issues you encounter in your EMDR therapy practice related to moving from Phase 2 into Phase 3?
- How can your own mindfulness practice assist in this critical decision-making process?
- What areas of the 11-step targeting sequence within the standard protocol do you find challenging?
- How might approaching the 11-step targeting sequence with a greater respect for the EMDR method as a mindfulness practice help you with your struggles?

REFERENCES

Abel, N., & O'Brien, J. M. (2014). *Treating addictions with EMDR and the stages of change.* New York, NY: Springer Publishing.

De Jongh, A., Resick, P. A., Zoellner, L. A., Van Minnen, A., Lee, C. W., Monson, C. M., . . . Bicanic, I. A. (2016). Critical analysis of the current treatment guidelines for complex PTSD in adults. *Depression and Anxiety, 33,* 359–369. doi:10.1002/da.22469

Goldstein, J. (2013). *Mindfulness: A practical guide to awakening.* Boulder, CO: Sounds True.

Hase, M. (2009). CraveEx: An EMDR approach to treat substance abuse and addiction. In M. Luber (Ed.), *Eye movement desensitization and reprocessing (EMDR) scripted protocols: Special populations* (pp. 467–488). New York, NY: Springer Publishing.

Kabat-Zinn, J. (2011). *Mindfulness for beginners: Reclaiming the present moment-and your life.* Boulder, CO: Sounds True Books.

Marich, J. (2011). *EMDR made simple: Four approaches to using EMDR with every client.* Eau Claire, WI: PESI Publishing (Premiere).

Markus, W., & Hornsveld, H. K. (2017). EMDR interventions in addiction. *Journal of EMDR Practice and Research, 11*(1), 3–29.

Miller, R. (2012). Treatment of behavioral addictions utilizing the feeling-state addiction protocol: A multiple base-line study. *Journal of EMDR Practice and Research, 6*(4), 159–169.

Parnell, L. (2007). *A therapist's guide to EMDR: Tools and techniques for successful treatment.* New York, NY: W. W. Norton.

Popky, A. J. (2005). DeTUR, an urge reduction protocol for addictions and dysfunctional behaviors. In R. Shapiro (Ed.), *EMDR solutions: Pathways to healing* (pp. 167–188). New York, NY: W. W. Norton.

Prochaska, J. O., & DiClemente, C. C. (1982). Transtheoretical therapy: Toward a more integrative model of change. *Psychotherapy: Theory, Research and Practice, 19*(3), 276–288.

Shapiro, F. (2001). *Eye movement desensitization and reprocessing: Basic principles, protocols, and procedures* (2nd ed.). New York, NY: Guilford Press.

Wise, A., & Marich, J. (2016). The perceived effects of standard and addiction-specific EMDR therapy protocols. *Journal of EMDR Practice and Research, 10*(4), 231–244.

8

Special Situations in Phases 3 to 6: Mindful Facilitation Through Abreaction, Dissociation, and Resistance

POTENTIAL FRUSTRATIONS IN EMDR THERAPY PHASES 3 TO 6

The transformative nature of EMDR therapy generally manifests in Phases 3 to 6. However, Phases 3 to 6 have the potential to trip up client and clinician alike. Abreactions are possible, reprocessing may stimulate a variety of tangential responses, and many clients simply get overwhelmed with affect. Shutting down or getting "stuck" are also common issues that emerge in Phases 3 to 6. Sometimes, these responses are reactions to the overwhelm; at other times the stalling happens before the proverbial train of reprocessing even leaves the station. With these frustrations, clients may end up declaring that "EMDR doesn't work" or "that EMDR thing we did is just too much." If a clinician is not equipped to handle this often-legitimate feedback, a client may dismiss EMDR therapy as an intervention going forward. Many clinicians initially trained in EMDR therapy end up abandoning it as an intervention, or feel forced to seek out other modalities in which to get training. Irritation can mount when situations continually arise in Phases 3 to 6 that do not quite correspond to textbook presentations or canned video demos of how EMDR therapy *should* work.

In this chapter, experience, strength, and hope in navigating the potential pitfalls commonly discussed in Phases 3 to 6 are presented. A major focus of our discussions is on how our personal mindfulness practices and calling upon mindfulness-informed strategies help clinicians to navigate these rough waters. You are challenged to consider how your personal mindfulness practice can help you maintain a calming presence during trauma reprocessing, more effectively equipping you to handle clinical curveballs and various manifestations of abreaction. The possibility of translating facets of personal mindfulness practice into a variety of interweave strategies is also explored. The chapter concludes by discussing how to work with clients who say that they do not want to "do" EMDR anymore, considering how the answers may lie in making necessary clinical adaptations and bolstering elements of mindful preparation.

MAINTAINING THE CALMING PRESENCE

The International Association for Trauma Professionals teaches that the therapist's ability to maintain a calming presence during sessions is one of the hallmarks of trauma-responsive care. Staying calm and not showing signs of nervousness, escalation, or dissociation on our part when we become worried about a client's response to an intervention is paramount. There is even a chance that the material a client is processing may trigger us, as clinicians, personally. Although it is important to notice how we are being triggered and come up with a plan to address that on our own time and in our own healing/self-care plan, in the moment we must be there for the client. Having a personal mindfulness practice will allow us to be there, be present, and be calm in the most effective way possible. Clinicians often teach this standard as a general expectation for trauma-focused care. Thus, it is vital for the EMDR therapist to acquire and to hone this competency of keeping calm and present amid adversity. We model to clients what we can put into practice for ourselves.

QUALITIES OF A GOOD EMDR THERAPIST

Laurel Parnell's (2007) six qualities of a good EMDR therapist, presented in *A Therapist's Guide to EMDR*, can be cultivated through active, personal mindfulness practice. Although the first two qualities she lists—good clinical skills and the ability to develop rapport with clients—are hopefully ubiquitous among therapists in general, the rest of the list takes on special importance to trauma therapists and specifically to EMDR therapists. Her third quality—being comfortable with trauma and intense affect—is paramount if you are going to effectively work with abreactions and signs of dissociation during Phases 3 to 6. The fourth quality—spaciousness—is a term often used in meditation and other New Age circles to suggest that we are not forcing our agendas on clients; rather, we are being a present witness for them to do the work that they need at the time. "Holding space" is a task that the EMDR therapist ought to take very seriously; our commitment to stay out of the way as much as possible to let the client do the work is the essence of what it means to hold space for someone. The fifth quality—being well-grounded—is what allows us to stay calm when a client abreacts or hits some other roadblock during reprocessing. If clinicians seriously commit to practicing and internalizing all the skills covered for grounding in previous chapters, we ought to have little problem staying grounded in sessions. The final quality—attunement to clients—is what allows EMDR therapists to read and artfully respond to nonverbal or energetic clues that clients may be giving us. Attunement, a word that has surged in clinical popularity in recent years with so much attention being paid to attachment, is at its heart a mindfulness practice. Attunement is what allows us to be more present in the EMDR therapy session and can help us to more effectively manage abreaction and dissociation when we see it, and know how to more artfully intervene with interweaves when they are needed.

MINDFUL SKILLS FOR THE JOURNEY THROUGH PHASES 3 TO 6

HANDLING ABREACTION AND DISSOCIATION

Shapiro (2001) prepares her readers for the likelihood of abreaction in EMDR therapy, although she also cautions that it is not a requirement for successful processing. Abreaction is a Freudian term that describes the often-intense discharge of emotion that accompanies material when it shifts from unconscious to conscious awareness. New EMDR therapists can easily feel that they have done something wrong when a client's abreaction is intense; an intensive abreaction or series of abreactions that catch them off guard or appear in a form they have not seen before can trip up even seasoned EMDR therapists. Not all abreactions are the stereotypical ugly cry or lashing out with a loud voice. Yawning and excessive displaying of tiredness can be a sign that the body and brain are overtaxed from these shifts in how emotions are stored. Laughter, especially if it seems ill-placed or defective, can also be a sign of abreaction, as can gastrointestinal events such as nausea, vomiting, or passing gas.

EMDR therapists are generally trained to orient clients to the possibility of abreactions. We inform clients that even though they have a right to stop processing and return to a safe anchor, the easiest way through an abreaction is likely to experience it in the context of the EMDR stimulation, intoning the folk knowledge that the easiest way out may be through.

There are two points of finesse in managing abreaction informed by our mindfulness practice. The first directly relates to attunement. Clients may never give us the stop sign or warning signal that they are near the edge of their affective window of tolerance. Many clients new to the reprocessing phases of EMDR therapy may be eager to have the EMDR work or eager to please us and, by not giving the stop sign or other warning, may end up overwhelming themselves too early in the process and not want to return.

A simple variation to use on "Go with that" is: "Are you okay to keep going?" This nuance is particularly effective if you determine that the client is near the edge of or outside the window of tolerance. Phrasing the question in this way, instead of "Would you like to stop or pause?" (although it may need to be that direct), reminds the client that the easiest way out may be through, although they are still empowered to stop. If, as part of your relationship building and orientation, you covered that it is important that clients not tell you what they think you want to hear, this strategy can be very effective. Adapt the feedback that you receive, either verbally or nonverbally, in accordance with the client and the overall flow of a session. Such feedback may suggest that the client needs shorter sets of eye movements and more frequent verbal check-ins.

The edict to EMDR therapists is to stay out of the way as much as possible. For clients who are new to the process, however, more frequent check-ins can have a grounding, stabilizing effect and a client may benefit from hearing your voice more frequently, even if it is through the simple, "What are you noticing now?" check-in. On the other side of this coin, some clients may require longer sets of the fast stimulation associated with reprocessing speed to really move through a component of their reprocessing. As long as clients are within their affective window of tolerance, there is no harm in applying longer sets (Bergmann, 2012). Being attuned to a client's process through your own mindful engagement with the session may help you to notice this, and adapt sets accordingly. If you are unsure, you can always clarify with the client using a line such as, "It seems to me like you may need me to let the stimulation go longer to really move through this material; what's your sense?"

A second approach for managing abreaction and signs of dissociation seems so simple, yet many EMDR therapists miss it: Taking a breath ourselves. Taking a deepened breath, generally a diaphragmatic breath or *ujjayi* breath (see Chapter 4), can have a remarkable effect on our ability to stay calm. The deepened breath can remind our bodies that we are in the presence of the session and that our breath continues to flow for us as our inherent resource for staying calm and grounded. Such breath can maintain or renew the clarity of our thought processes when difficult situations arise in EMDR therapy sessions. Moreover, the deepened breath, particularly if we are bringing some subtle sound into it, like in *ujjayi* breath, can model for the client the importance of breath and serve as an indirect reminder to keep the breath flowing as deeply as possible. So many clients that struggle with intense affect and emotion do so because they are straining to clench their muscles and hold their breath.

A variation on "the easiest way out may be through" is that the easiest way to ride out an emotional experience is to let your breath help you. Jon Kabat-Zinn, the great secular mindfulness teacher and developer of Mindfulness-Based Stress Reduction (MBSR) often uses the metaphor that you cannot stop the waves from coming, but you can learn how to surf. There are few other modern metaphors that so beautifully capture how a mindfulness practice can benefit a client's flow in EMDR Phases 3 through 6. Several EMDR therapists in our circles will often use the encouraging statement, "Ride the wave," along with a deep breath as intense affect and emotion surfaces in EMDR Phase 4. This subtle interweave, inspired by Kabat-Zinn and Marsha Linehan's own interpretation of mindfulness in dialectal behavior therapy, truly represents the essence of mindful EMDR therapy.

The strategy of using our own breath as a reminder to the client is generally most effective when mindfulness and breath work are used in Phase 2, Preparation. Too often when clinicians simply tell their clients to "remember to breathe" or "just take a deep breath," they can look at us blankly or comment—verbally or nonverbally—that "just breathing" is much easier said than done. Even the preferred method for many of us for checking in after stimulation—"Take a breath; what are you noticing now?"—works best when a client has had a chance in the Preparation phase to practice the art of taking a breath and noticing their experience. If the first time the client is hearing that line or some variation of it is in Phase 4, it is generally too late.

Many of the same preparatory strategies suggested for working with abreaction are also effective in managing signs of dissociation in Phases 3 to 6. As with abreaction, it is important to consider that dissociation can take on many forms, not just flipping between parts and ego states. Nor is dissociation only the act of zoning out, though that may happen in various degrees. Physical tension (watch for the shoulders creeping toward the ears), looking up, looking away, or not being able to verbalize during a check-in (especially when there is little noticeable sign of affect) are all potential signals. Similar to the logic of working with abreaction, just because you as the EMDR therapist are seeing signs of dissociation in Phase 4 does not mean you must stop reprocessing. Rather, go to your safeguards that were hopefully developed during Phase 2 (more on this in Chapter 6). For some, a simple check-in with grounding, which you can invite at any time during the reprocessing more as a pause than as a full stop, will suffice. Shortening the sets or switching to another mode of stimulation that helps the client to feel more present and "in the room" may help. Finally, never underestimate the importance of modeling the breath. *Ujjayi* breath ("ocean sounding victory" breath) is recommended. The sound element involved with this breath can add an additional sensory layer to the phenomenon of grounding. Additionally, the actions involved with *ujjayi* breath have a directly stimulative effect on the vagus nerve, which can promote parasympathetic rest or relaxation. If doing this kind of breath during Phase 4 is the first time you are introducing it, know that it may be too late to have much impact in the moment without some practice. Reemphasizing a major theme of this book, consider that a mindful, well-attended Preparation phase will serve you and your client well in these later phases.

Rochelle is an EMDR therapy client who benefits significantly from regular work with breath to prevent abreactions from turning to overwhelm. Diagnosed with PTSD and generally conceptualized as a case of complex PTSD due to the impact of childhood sexual trauma perpetrated by a family member, Rochelle initially found relief from her symptoms through basic coping strategies and active participation in sports. However, an unexpected physical health problem that developed in her mid-thirties significantly impacted her mobility and, as she became less active, her old symptoms of PTSD returned: primarily intense panic, flashbacks (with significant dissociative components), and physiological disturbance. Rochelle presented for EMDR therapy after experiencing some initial relief from her symptoms through practicing yoga, so she was very open to working with breath throughout her EMDR therapy process.

When Rochelle began to show first signs of intensified distress and dissociation during Phase 4 reprocessing, her eyes would wander off to the farthest corner of the room. At this point, she would begin to have difficulty tracking. This was her EMDR therapist's signal to take a deep *ujjayi* breath, which would encourage Rochelle to do the same. In some sets, taking the one breath was enough to get Rochelle back on track with reprocessing. At other times, the EMDR therapist's initiation of the *ujjayi* breath would prompt Rochelle to pause the eye movements and continue with several repetitions of *ujjayi* breathing, a sign that she needed more time to pause and to ground. When Rochelle became ready, she would shift from the breath to make eye contact with her therapist, and the sets of stimulation would commence. Although still an active EMDR therapy client, Rochelle reports significant shifts in her overall trauma-based symptomatology, including a near elimination in what she describes as "breakdowns" when reminded of her primary abuser. She reports a decrease in flashbacks and an overall improved ability to remain calm when she is encountered with reminders of her abuse. Rochelle was previously unable to tolerate the emotion whenever she heard a name spoken that was close to her abuser's name. She considers the elimination of this phenomenon to be a major benefit of her work with EMDR therapy, work that she reports being able to tolerate because of how breath is used in the process.

INTERWEAVES

For mindfulness practitioners, Shapiro's emphasis to "stay out of the way" as much as possible in EMDR therapy holds great appeal. This teaching also offers evidence to just how mindfulness-infused the practice of EMDR really is at its core. Yet most mindfulness practitioners have found themselves in stuck places within their practice where just the right teaching, the seemingly inspired directive, can infuse our practice and get us back on track. Shapiro's development of cognitive interweaves, or the open-ended questions or statements clinicians can utilize in the flow of EMDR therapy in any phase to assist clients through blocks in processing, parallels this phenomenon. Interweaves ought to be used sparingly and only after several sets of encouraging a client to "go with that" have not resulted in much desensitization or movement. However, the more complexities clients may face—difficulty staying on track, problems paying attention, issues with emotionally blocking, or general "resistance"—the more interweave they may require. There is a parallel to mindfulness practice in general, particularly with beginners, and how a skillful teacher can guide their journey. Many people can begin and maintain a mindfulness practice on their own with the aid of books, apps, or other instructions. Most people find it difficult to have a sitting practice on their own, and many are stymied by the first time or first few times that they cannot maintain concentration. In those cases, new practitioners are encouraged to find a teacher and a community where they can taste different practices and be given practices tailored to their particular challenges. Silent meditation without good guides can devolve into rumination or escape fantasy. A teacher can offer guidance, even guided meditations, to provide the structure necessary for a beginner or one who is struggling.

Not all effective interweaves are necessarily cognitive, which is why the general term "interweave" is preferred by many EMDR therapy practitioners. A common interweave to use, inspired by some of Shapiro's own writing, is "What are you noticing in your body now?" Although clinicians use the cognitive channel to activate the question, the interweave is essentially somatic in nature. Sometimes, clinicians can convey the spirit of such an interweave, inviting the client into the body, by taking that deep, voluminous breath to model breathing for the client. With this strategy, the EMDR therapist is technically intervening, although in a subtle way where no words have to be exchanged. Some of your clients may require more directive, creative interweaves such as taking movement or expressive-arts breaks, inspired by some of the skills covered in Chapter 4. While more traditional EMDR therapists may advise such styles of interweave only for children (and the canon on EMDR for children advises such creative modification), some of these same strategies work beautifully for the stuck adult, too! If you understand how ego states can interplay with each other, the idea of applying to adults the creativity we use with children ought to make perfect sense. If it does not, consider seeking further consultation. If you are an EMDR therapist who works primarily with adults, you may even derive benefit from working with an EMDR consultant who works primarily with children and is well-attuned to these creative modifications. Any modification that is made for children may be a good fit for the stuck child states within your adult clients, or the expressive organicity of how we work with children may translate well to the creative adult.

The more diligently you develop a personal mindfulness practice in concert with practicing your EMDR therapy skills, the more effectively and artfully you will be able to use interweaves when people are stuck. As long as you consider the teaching that the operative is to "stay out of the way" as much as possible, you are respecting the spirit of using interweaves only when needed. When the situation arises for an interweave, how can you present what you may be observing in a way that steers the client further down the path while still honoring that the path is the client's, not your own? You are simply the guide. If you are observing that the client is stuck or looping in one channel of processing, how might you use the art of the interweave to elicit the wisdom that can be found in another channel? Although exceptions exist, the best interweaves to serve this purpose are open-ended questions, as in the examples offered in Exhibit 8.1.

Abreaction and dissociation must not be feared. With mindfulness and the safety created by containment, EMDR therapists can deal with each of these types of reactions. These reactions are not mandatory; moreover, it is not a sign of failure if they are not present. However, they can become powerful aspects of the mindful reprocessing experiences. Spencer, an EMDR therapist who extensively studied Zen earlier in his life, reflected:

One morning while on retreat I found myself in a state of abreaction, a flood of tears that had what seemed like a number of sources. When I went for my interview with the teacher that morning, I told him what had been happening, that I could not stop crying on the cushion all morning long. His reply: "When you have cried half as many tears as I have, you will be well on your way to enlightenment."

EXHIBIT 8.1 Quick Reference Table: Mindful Interweaves in EMDR Therapy

- **Client:** "I'm just not feeling anything right now."
  - *What does that mean to you that you're not feeling anything?*
  - *So if you can't feel, what are you thinking about right now?*
  - *What was the last thing that you noticed before the feeling stopped?*
- **Client:** "I start to feel something, then I just shut down or get distracted."
  - *What was so troubling/disturbing about the last thing that you felt before you shut down?*
  - *What does it mean to you to be distracted or to shut down?*
  - *Thinking over the course of your whole life, when did you seem to develop this shutting-down response?*
- **Client:** "I just want to make sense of it all" (or similar reports evidencing cognitive-only focus without emotional or somatic connection).
  - *How does it feel that you can't make sense of it all?*
  - *What does that mean to you that you can't make sense of it all?*
  - *What's happening in your body right now as you're going through all these thoughts?*
  - *How has that worked for you so far just trying to think it through?*
- **Client:** "I got nothing/Nothing is happening."
  - *Nothing as in numb, or nothing as in all clear?*
  - *What does nothing feel like in your body?*
  - *Is your body trying to protect you from something?*
  - *What is the last thing you remember noticing before you went into "nothing"?*
  - *Could it be that you're trying to make sense of it all, instead of just letting the feelings and sensations come up on their own?*
- **Client:** "I don't think that this EMDR thing is working."
  - *What makes you think/say it's not working?*
  - *How does it feel to you when something doesn't work?*
  - *What does that mean to you when something isn't working?*
- **Client:** "I just feel so <u>guilty</u> about the whole thing" (same thing comes up for several consecutive sets—a looping response).
  - *What does <u>guilt</u> mean to you? (adjust underlined word based on what's looping)*
  - *What does being <u>guilty</u> say about you?*

(continued)

EXHIBIT 8.1 Quick Reference Table: Mindful Interweaves in EMDR Therapy (*Continued*)

> ○ *Where do you seem to experience/feel that <u>guilt</u> the strongest in your body?*
> ○ *Does this <u>guilt</u> about this incident we're working on remind you of how you felt at an earlier time in your life? (if the guilt or looped report is present-focused)*

Abreaction is just another aspect of experience on which to apply mindful concentration, and more is revealed by allowing it to be exactly as it is. The same logic applies with dissociation. Zen *koan* practice was developed as a spiritual tool for mindfulness practitioners. In a sense, these Zen stories or statements are designed to give your rational mind something to wrestle with that is unsolvable from that perspective—in a sense, promoting dissociation (Loori, 2005). There are other Buddhist mindfulness techniques that do the same. In EMDR therapy, clinicians engage with dissociation in a similar fashion, yet in a much safer, more therapeutically driven manner: we provide interweaves when necessary, we provide additional grounding when needed. And still, we stay out of the way as much as possible.

"I DON'T WANT TO DO EMDR ANYMORE"

"I don't think this is working" is one of many protestations that EMDR therapist consultants hear from both frustrated clients and frustrated consultees. Clinicians can see EMDR work a certain way in online demonstrations or during their training experience, and then get frustrated when roadblocks appear in actual clinical life. If you have experienced this frustration as a new EMDR clinician, please know that you are not alone. It can be extremely difficult to learn a new approach to psychotherapy, especially one that arguably has more in common with mindfulness meditation than it does with talk therapy. To summarize a major theme in this chapter and throughout the book, cultivating your own mindfulness practice can help with this process of learning to keep a calming presence, particularly as you learn something new. Mindfulness practice can also help you stay out of the way with your clients as is advised in EMDR therapy, yet also navigate the unplanned scenarios where you may have to intervene. Just as advocating a great deal of preparation for your own clients is recommended, preparation on your part, even if that means diving into the practices and principles covered in Chapters 3 to 5, is essential. Even if you are a seasoned EMDR clinician who has moved past the beginner's nervousness about dealing with the unexpected, bolstering your own mindfulness practice may prove to be the most fruitful path you have ever trod toward strengthening your abilities in EMDR therapy.

Many clients proclaim that EMDR therapy is just too much for them, that they do not want to do it again. When clients say that they do not want to do EMDR therapy any more or simply refuse to come back (a topic covered more fully in the next chapter), it is often because the experience of Phases 3 to 4 or the full Phases 3 to 6 proved too emotionally or somatically overwhelming. The more experience you have with blending EMDR therapy and mindfulness, the more accustomed you will become to meeting such feedback in a way that validates client frustration or overwhelm, yet also helps them to feel safe enough to explore what might have happened. Two case studies published by Chinese practitioners reported that the EMDR therapy itself seemed to be too intensive for the clients in question: a 38-year-old male Taiwanese civil servant (Tzan-Fu & Nien-Mu, 2007) and an elderly patient with depression awaiting a medical procedure (Sun, Wu, & Chiu, 2004). Integrating mindfulness meditation training, which included many of the practices described in Chapter 3, seemed to make the EMDR more tolerable for the clients and allowed positive results to be experienced.

Often, the sense of overwhelm that leads client to balk at EMDR therapy directly corresponds to insufficient preparation and inadequate closure. The next chapter goes into further detail on how assuring a strong closure, usually made possible through a solid preparation, is vital. A mindful EMDR therapist is able and willing to take feedback from a client about what did not work for the client and adapt accordingly, which usually means returning to the Preparation phase and/or readjusting the target that you work on first in Phases 3 to 6.

TYING IT ALL TOGETHER

The Buddha provided several foundational teachings regarding mindfulness. One he called the three characteristics of existence: impermanence, suffering/unsatisfactoriness, and something he called not-self or no-self. As these relate to EMDR therapy and trauma therapy in general, they speak to our role as a therapist. First, EMDR therapists stay out of the way as much as possible, allowing for the impermanent flow of reprocessing to occur, our own mindfulness working with the mindfulness of the client to maintain this spirit of allowing and noticing. In addition, our role as therapist is that of developing wisdom regarding suffering, and then pointing our skills and our mindfulness toward the suffering in order to relieve it. Therefore, it will be advantageous to lose or tame our ego as much as possible. Mindfulness teaches us the same premise that Shapiro does: that we are only facilitators of a process, we are not the agent of change. With a dedicated mindfulness practice of our own, we can let go of our own attachments to clinical outcomes, the paradox being that the clinical outcomes improve as we step out of the way. Mark Epstein (2007), the Buddhist psychiatrist, said we can provide "psychotherapy without the self." That is the EMDR therapist at work, allowing the possibility of the client's own experience providing the healing, much like the Buddha suggested almost 2,600 years ago that we might experience ourselves.

QUESTIONS FOR REFLECTION AND PERSONAL PRACTICE

- What are your experiences with how integrating breath into your own life helps with grounding and moving the flow along?

- How do you translate skills you have learned about the breath personally to how you deliver EMDR therapy?

- What types of fears around abreaction, complex trauma, and dissociation still exist for you? How might personal mindfulness practice help you to address some of these fears?

- What struggles do you have with "staying out of the way" in EMDR therapy? Do you tend to over-rely on interweaves or not use them enough? How can mindfulness help you to strike a balance in the application of interweaves?

REFERENCES

Bergmann, U. (2012). *Neurobiological foundations for EMDR practice.* New York, NY: Springer Publishing.

Epstein, M. (2007). *Psychotherapy without the self: A Buddhist perspective.* New Haven, CT: Yale University Press.

Loori, J. (2005). *Sitting with koans: Essential writings on Zen koan introspection.* Boston, MA: Wisdom Publications.

Parnell, L. (2007). *A therapist's guide to EMDR: Tools and techniques for successful treatment.* New York, NY: W. W. Norton.

Shapiro, F. (2001). *Eye movement desensitization and reprocessing: Basic principles, protocols, and procedures* (2nd ed.). New York, NY: Guilford Press.

Sun, T. F., Wu, C. K., & Chiu, N. M. (2004). Mindfulness meditation training combined with eye movement desensitization and reprocessing in psychotherapy of an elderly patient. *Chang Gung Medical Journal, 27*(6), 464–469.

Tzan-Fu, S., & Nien-Mu, C. (2006). Synergism between mindfulness meditation training, and eye movement desensitization and reprocessing in psychotherapy of social phobia. *Chang Gung Medical Journal, 29*(4), 1–4.

9

EMDR Phases 7 and 8: Mindfully Approaching What We Often Overlook

THE MINDFUL PRACTICE OF TRANSITION

In the "Dancing Mindfulness" practice and in many other expressive arts therapy practices, the idea of honoring transition is cherished. For instance, if you are doing a stretch sequence on the ground and the facilitator (or the music) tells you that it is time to come up to your feet, avoid simply jumping up to your feet. Let moving to your feet from the ground be a process; allow the transition to become part of the dance. With more traditional mindfulness practice, you may be in a sitting meditation practice for an extended period when the teacher rings a bell or the timer you have set for yourself indicates that time is up. It is generally unwise to just hop up and move on to the next thing on your schedule. In the first few moments after the bell, what do you experience when you fully allow for transitions? If your eyes are closed or in a soft gaze, perhaps you allow them to blink and adjust to the light. Maybe you move or wiggle in your chair or on your cushion to notice your body after being in stillness for such a long time. Allowing for these small movements may be an important part of how you check in with your grounding, particularly if the period of meditation was challenging. You may also need to scan the room as a transition, noticing what you see, what you smell, what you observe. If you practice yoga or any other type of spiritual or contemplative practice, this idea of honoring the importance of transition hopefully resonates.

TRANSITIONS IN EMDR THERAPY

Taking your time with transitions is likely something you have experienced in your life, in one form or another. As with many facets of mindfulness, honoring transition may strike us as a radical idea, especially in modern times where rushing from one task to the next is often the norm. The transition may not seem as exciting as the outcome or end result, yet there is much to be learned in savoring it. Both Phases 7 and 8 of EMDR therapy offer the client and clinician critical opportunities for transition. Too often these phases do not get the attention that they deserve, even among experienced EMDR therapists. Phase 7, Closure, facilitates transition from one session to the next. Closure allows the client to more adaptively transition from the clinical session back to daily life. Phase 8, Reevaluation, provides a plethora of opportunities for transition from one target to the next, ultimately bringing about a sense of wholeness to the treatment experience.

Phases 7 and 8 are addressed together in this chapter through the lens of mindful transition. In this chapter, we explore how clinicians and clients can optimize the efficacy of the Closure phase by approaching it as a mindfulness practice. We also explore how revisiting mindfulness practices developed in Phase 2, Preparation, will allow clients to leave clinical settings in as safe a manner as possible and more effectively manage affect in between sessions. Mindfulness practices help clinicians to increase their flexibility and openness to moving with the flow of a client's treatment. Approaching Phase 7 with this flexibility is vital. Further working with these qualities of flow and flexibility will likely usher in a new appreciation for Phase 8 and its implications for trauma-focused treatment planning.

TRANSITION AS MINDFULNESS PRACTICE: AN EXPLORATORY EXERCISE

Before moving along with this chapter, you are encouraged to take a few moments to practice what it means to honor transition. By engaging in this activity you will not only get a chance to cultivate another dimension of your personal mindfulness practice, you will also be able to more fully appreciate this chapter's presentation of Phases 7 and 8. You are encouraged and welcome to modify this practice for use with clients.

- Choose a mindfulness practice from Chapters 3 or 4 for this experimentation.

- Set a timer for the desired length of practice (a minimum of five minutes is recommended).

- Engage in the practice as you have learned it.

- When the timer rings, resist any temptation to immediately stop the timer and rush on to the next thing you have scheduled. Take at least 30 seconds to listen to the ring of the timer.

- After you have stopped the timer, whether your eyes are closed or in a soft gaze, give yourself several minutes to really look around the room. Notice what you see, what you smell, what you observe, scanning as many of your sensory experiences as possible.

- If you chose a seated or still mindfulness practice, give yourself at least 30 seconds to stretch or engage in some organic movement. If you chose a moving or more creative mindfulness exercise, give yourself at least 30 seconds to notice the stillness after the movement.

- Take as much time as you need to experience these moments of transition before moving along to your next practice, returning to work, or proceeding with your next activity for the day.

FURTHER MODIFICATIONS AND OPTIONS FOR CREATIVITY

○ If you truly want to play with the possibilities of transition, consider stringing together three to five of your favorite mindfulness practices covered in Chapters 3 and 4, taking your time with transition, as described in the main exercise.

○ For optimal challenge, set an intention to combine some of the practices you like and some of the practices you find more difficult. Notice the role that honoring the transition plays in being able to tolerate distress or discomfort.

○ In working with children or clients who need more modifications, brainstorm for a word that works better than "transition" to capture the essence of this practice.

PHASE 7: CLOSURE

LEARNING FROM MISTAKES

From the inception of EMDR, Shapiro emphasized the importance of safely closing sessions. Her 2001 textbook covers what she sees as the fundamental components of closure—preparing a client for what may happen in between sessions (e.g., processing may continue), developing a plan for handling residual distress that may heighten in between sessions, reviewing any other safety-planning elements (e.g., reaching out to a support system or a therapist on call), and answering any client questions or concerns. Many EMDR practitioners can rush through the Closure phase—and even the most seasoned of EMDR therapists and consultants are willing to admit to it. A major reason for it can stem from wanting to maximize our available reprocessing time in sessions; clinicians who need to practice in the 45- or 50-minute hour can feel enslaved by this time crunch. Many EMDR therapists have experienced the pressure of sensing that a client is close to resolving any given target to a SUDs (subjective units of distress) of 0 and VoC (validity of cognition) of 7, and believe that just one or two more sets ought to suffice. Then, a client can turn an unexpected corner in processing and a whole new channel gets opened up as the session runs close to the end. Moreover, some major material may prove to be what prevents a SUDs of 1 from clearing fully to 0. There seems to be an unspoken shame among EMDR therapists around not completing targets. To emphasize, it is permissible to close down incomplete sessions, especially if you work in traditional practices with time constraints. It is much safer to effectively close a session, give the client a chance to practice using skills in life in between sessions, and then resume the work in a subsequent session.

Being a mindful EMDR therapist does not only require one to be mindful of time and context, it also means being able to make clinical decisions on a case-by-case basis. Some clients may need more of a closure ritual than others. In the first few sessions of reprocessing, spend at least 10 minutes on closure; with certain complex or dissociative clients, up to 15 minutes may be warranted. You will learn from clients how much or how little time they may need to close down a session as you continue to work with them. This practice of closure can become an art form as EMDR therapists learn more about how to respect the phase as a transition.

Another common mistake made by EMDR therapists at every level of experience is underestimating a client's need for closure, and reviewing a safety plan. You may relate to this experience from your practice: A first reprocessing session seems to go perfectly, textbook even. There is a complete resolution of a target to a SUDs of 0 and a VoC of 7, and in the session debrief the client reports feeling splendid! Then, a client may not come back for the next session, or contacts you frantically to report being an emotional wreck since the session. These situations often happen because even though a target seems to resolve, a client has not been adequately prepared for the phenomenon that processing can continue in between sessions. Heavy emotions connected to other targets still needing to be addressed can emerge and a variety of responses can result. Some clients become so overwhelmed that they forget to access their skills. Other clients become so confident by the instruction to "go with that" they may try diving into more of their own processing without guidance in between sessions.

Although these kinds of responses are expected with clients new to EMDR therapy, even clients who have been in treatment long term and are used to how EMDR sessions work still benefit from closure. With many long-term clients, continue to invite some type of closure ritual. The ritual or practice can be something as simple as taking three deep cleansing breaths (see *Ritual Release Breathing* at the end of this section), or "shaking off" any residual distressed noticed in the body, returning it to the earth (see the *Noodling* practice in Chapter 4 and test out a new practice, *Flicking*, at the end of this section). Following up one of these simple practices with a statement such as, "Do you have any questions about self-care in between sessions or about anything that happened today?" is also recommended with your long-term clients. Even for clients who consistently maintain that they are okay, your willingness to remind them about closure serves as excellent modeling about respecting the practice of transition.

Ritual Release Breathing: A Simple Breath Practice for EMDR Closure

This exercise is inspired by a character in Stephen King's classic *The Green Mile*. If you saw the film, you may remember how the mystical John Coffey would breathe out a swarm of pests after he healed someone with his magical touch. More specifically, he would tilt his head back and make an audible breath as he could see the distress leave his body. Although you do not have to make a reference to John Coffey if you or your clients are not familiar with the book/film, you can still facilitate this skill as a breath visualization.

- Notice your body in this moment. Pay attention: is there any distress or tension still lingering?

- Tilt your head back slightly.

- Inhale deeply with your nose, allowing the belly to expand gently as in diaphragmatic breath.

- As you exhale, open your mouth widely and make a sound.

- Visualize any distress or tension that you noticed leaving your body. What color is that distress or tension? If you like, you can also imagine that the distress has a texture, like thick smog or some other unpleasant element. Use your imagination.

- Repeat this as many times as necessary until you experience that enough of the tension has left your body to feel okay to go.

Further Modifications and Options for Creativity

o Many clients will recognize the John Coffey reference, and bringing this up may do half the work. If not, you will likely have to use the detail in this script to help a client fully develop the visualization. You can invite clients to bring in their own movie or mythical references if they have them to develop this technique.

o This visualization breath is best done with clients who have worked with breath on some level in Preparation phase. This specific skill can be taught and practiced during Preparation, although it can have special application as a closure strategy.

o There are numerous implications for art-making with this skill. You can invite clients to use pens, colored pencils, pastels, or other art-making materials to draw their visualization of the breath they wish to release.

o This breath is a fabulous self-care strategy for clinicians to use, especially if you only have a few quick moments of changeover in between sessions. Even if a session did not register for you as particularly difficult, remember that any session has a potential to impact your body. Consider how consistently working with this breath and accompanying visualization throughout the day can help you with your own cleansing and releasing.

Flicking: A Simple Energy Practice for EMDR Closure

When your therapeutic session is ending, consider using the following steps as a closure ritual or strategy. The purpose of the skill is to encourage clients to cast off and leave behind any residual stress, anxiety, or body distress from the session.

• Take a moment and come to a place of stillness. Once you are still, notice the breath. You can simply track the breath in-and-out, or engage one of your favorite strategies for deepening your breath.

• Notice if any residual or lingering distress is noticeable in your body. If it helps you to think of that distress having a color, a shape, a texture, or a temperature, you can notice those.

• Imagine that this lingering distress is moving to both of your hands.

• Begin the motion of "flicking" this energetic representation of the distress out of your hands, as if you are purposely shaking off or casting off water after you have washed your hands.

• If it helps, tune into the sound that your fingers are making as you "flick" the distress away from you.

- Consciously "flick" or send the distress from your hands down to the direction of the earth. In Native American and many other indigenous traditions, the earth is regarded as a place where negative energy can be absorbed and transformed.

- Continue this process as much as you need with the intention of sending to the earth and leaving behind any lingering distress from the session.

- Know that you can repeat this exercise as often as needed in between sessions.

FURTHER MODIFICATIONS AND OPTIONS FOR CREATIVITY

○ This practice can be done sitting or standing. Standing may be preferred to assist with the grounding potential of the exercise and to serve as a true transition from sitting down in therapy to leaving the office and returning to the world.

○ "Flicking" is a practice that lends itself well to being done bilaterally or with dual attention. Your client can flick with the right hand and then the left, in alternating fashion.

○ Work with your clients to develop words and concepts for this closing release exercise that may best serve them. Some clients prefer the concept of "shaking off" or "leaving behind" more than "flicking." Similarly, if using such words as "energy" or "bad vibes" does not work with your client's spiritual belief system, ask which words or concepts might work. Simple phrases such as "I'm sending away the bad stuff" may work just fine!

○ Some clients prefer to "flick" or send their distress up to the sky, specifically if they conceptualize their Higher Power or spiritual presence to be up in the heavens. This modification is acceptable if the client releases residual distress with the intention of their Higher Power receiving it. Otherwise, clients may be bothered by the notion later that the stress is still lingering in the air around them.

BEST PRACTICES FOR MINDFUL CLOSURE

Doing your clinical work well in Phase 2, Preparation, will serve you in closure. Many of the skills in Phase 2—orienting the client for the journey ahead, developing a set of skills for grounding and distress tolerance, and assuring for a solid working therapeutic relationship are revisited in Phase 7. One of the many reasons we emphasize spending quality time on cultivating mindfulness skills in Phase 2 is so that they will be at your client's disposal to use in closure and beyond (e.g., in between sessions, after treatment terminates). It may even be worthwhile for you to go back and review Chapters 3, 4, and 6. Consider the implications that each skill carries in the Closure phase. In this section, the three essential components of closure are covered: closing and debriefing a session with a client, implementing a safety plan for in between sessions, and working with extraordinary circumstances.

Closing and Debriefing a Session

A client always has a right to come back to a preparation skill (e.g., Calm Safe Place, Light Stream, container, another meditation or strategy) as part of the closure process. Truly, any of the skills covered throughout the book can work in closure. In the case of incomplete sessions, working with the container strategy can be especially useful, even if implemented in combination with another skill. An example of this combination could be inviting clients to visualize the force of their favorite breath strategy closing and sealing the container. For clients new to EMDR therapy who may still be tentative about speaking up for what they need, you as the clinician may remind them that these strategies can be used in closure. As the clinician, keeping in a prominent place a running list of strategies, skills, and meditations that a client finds helpful can assist in the process of closure.

For some clients, the simple act of conversation can be a vital part of the closure process. Because EMDR therapy Phases 3 to 6 emphasize noticing and sensing more than talking or analyzing, a client's lower brain may still be activated when the time comes to wrap up a session. Although many of the skills emphasized in this book and in others on EMDR therapy can help with quelling significant visceral activation, the simple act of just talking can move a person back into primary activation in the neocortex. The process of conversation as transition can take on several qualities and carry many benefits. Some clients, especially those new to the EMDR therapy process, have legitimate questions about what they just experienced. Your willingness to answer these questions within the context of your therapeutic relationship can be incredibly normalizing and balancing to the client. Ensure that your session debriefs do not devolve into talk therapy. However, sharing an insight or two about how you experienced the session can nicely transition to reviewing a plan for managing distress in between sessions. On a lighter note, never underestimate the power of general, colloquial conversation about something that interests the client during the Closure phase. For example, some clients are best served by talking about sports in the last five minutes of the session and telling their therapist about what games they plan on watching that weekend. Maybe you have had a client who describes hiking plans for the following day, complete with specific descriptions of the landscape. This specificity about something completely unrelated to their trauma can promote a sense of grounding and stability before leaving the session.

Implementing a Safety Plan for In Between Sessions

There is a delicate balance that EMDR therapists must strike between alerting clients to the distress they may experience in between sessions and not painting too gloomy a picture. Some clients may develop a fear of proceeding with EMDR therapy if they hear that life is going to get worse because of what gets stirred up by EMDR. Clinicians must be careful not to unrealistically portray EMDR therapy, especially to complex clients, as a panacea that is going to wipe out the traumatic memories in short order. It is unfair to tell clients, "Just go to your skills and you'll be fine," when there is a real chance for distress to get more intense for a while before it clears. This risk is heightened when a client is able to take part in a 45- to 50-minute session only once a week. The balance you can strike is letting clients know that opening traumatic memories for processing may involve emotions becoming more awakened in between sessions. Remind clients that they can go over as many skills as they may need to assist them in managing these emotions, reminding them to keep their eyes on the prize of whatever ultimate goal led them to therapy.

For clients new to EMDR therapy, directly encouraging them to write down a list of their distress tolerance or other coping skills in their journal, on a note card, or using the note feature on their smartphone is warranted. One of the last activities you may consider covering in preparation for the reprocessing phases is to work with a client on making such a list. Collaborating on this exercise offers a powerful opportunity for orientation to both the potential intensity of Phases 3 to 6 and how using the developed strategies can empower a client to manage that intensity. Although making a simple list of skills can work, Exhibit 9.1 offers an example of how you can help a client to take the exercise a step further by planning ahead for specifics.

Processing may continue after any given EMDR session ends; this can come in the form of continued thoughts, somatic experiences, surfacing of new memories, or vivid dreams. For some clients, normalizing these responses can be enough to help them manage; others will need a clearly spelled-out plan of action. Clinical judgment is required in helping clients develop such action plans. Some clients may be adequately resourced and feel stable enough to employ such methods as journaling, art making,

EXHIBIT 9.1 Coping Skills and Emotional Management Plan: Sandy (Sample Client From Chapter 5)

POTENTIAL DISTRESS OR SITUATION	SKILL(S) TO USE
Seeing women who remind me of my mother	Ocean breathing, container exercise, leaving the situation if possible
Getting angry (often happens with no specific trigger)	Clench-and-release exercise, chopping wood outside, calling a friend/recovery support
Being overwhelmed at work	Going outside regularly to get fresh air, making sure to leave on time, ocean breathing, taking a drink of ice water, listening to music on the way home or on breaks (if possible)
Feeling like I'm going to cry, especially related to loneliness	Breath-tracking practice, feeling tone meditation, going outside
Cravings to drink	Calling someone in recovery support system (friend Randall; cousin Danielle), talking to a bandmate; going outside and taking a walk and making an effort to smell the air, a plant, the ground

movement practices, or extended periods in seated meditations to help them continue noticing experiences.

Many clients demonstrate significant potential to use such practices to continue their own work connecting the dots in between sessions, maximizing what we are able to do in the sessions themselves. Some clients may feel overwhelmed trying practices like these on their own, at least during their initial exposures to EMDR reprocessing. Thus, it may be wiser to emphasize containment, grounding, and distress tolerance in the time between sessions. You can encourage clients to make notes of what might be coming up for them from one session to the next, yet caution against intense exploration on their own. The more you commit to your own practice of mindfulness in EMDR therapy, the more effectively you will be able to handle these clinical judgment calls. Because it is not feasible to account for every possible contingency, having some arrangement for the client to contact you after their first few sessions to check in about what is working and what is not may be advisable (more on this in the next section).

Having a list of people to call is a time-honored coping-skill suggestion in 12-step recovery programs. When a person first attends meetings, they are encouraged to collect as many phone numbers as possible to build potential outlets for support. Sometimes, just the act of dialing the numbers can be a therapeutic exercise, even if it takes you a while to reach someone. Much of this same therapeutic value can be applied to working with mental health and trauma. Many EMDR clinicians feel better about proceeding with reprocessing if clients have at least one person they can call in between sessions if they need a listening ear. See Chapter 6 for more information on helping clients build and cultivate support, including the limitations encountered by some of our clients in this area and how to address those limitations. If clients do not have specific people to whom they feel comfortable reaching out between sessions, consider familiarizing yourself with available crisis lines in your area or nationally. If you employ an answering service or work for an agency with an on-call service, consider how employing these resources can be helpful for clients who are newly discovering how they respond to EMDR therapy.

Extraordinary Circumstances in Closure

Clinician policies vary on phone, e-mail, or text contact, so you will have to field these suggestions in the context of what works for you and your setting. Whatever your policies are regarding phone contact, which may include use of an answering service or agency crisis line, review them with your clients. Most clients new to EMDR therapy feel reassured by the knowledge that they can call if something unexpected or distressing emerges following their first few sessions of reprocessing.

As Mae, a former EMDR therapy client, noted, the material that surfaced during the EMDR sessions was intricately connected to her addiction relapse triggers. The fact that her clinician cared enough to remind her in every EMDR session closure to use the agency crisis line if needed served as a powerful rapport-building strategy for Mae. This reminder showed Mae that her EMDR therapist cared about her, and as their bond deepened, so did the depth of the work Mae was able to undertake (Marich, 2010).

As a safety check for clients that you assess to be more complicated, it may be a good idea to call or e-mail them the day after their first processing session. You do not have to make a habit of this after every session, but if you are willing it can serve as a solid safety measure and continued orientation gesture for your clients. As it was in Mae's case, this practice may help advance your therapeutic relationship with the client. For complex clients and those with dissociative risks, especially during their first few sessions of reprocessing, it may be wise as a safety measure to schedule them last on your calendar for that day. Minimally, have some type of agreement where they can sit in a waiting room or another office until they feel ready to leave. If you practice in an office without an area suitable for waiting, you can encourage people to sit outside or in their car listening to music or meditating in silence as long as they may need before leaving. Other possible safety measures include having another person bring a client to sessions until it is clear how the client will respond to EMDR therapy, or planning not to go back to work or school after a session, at least initially. As with every other component of EMDR therapy, these safety practices are open to reevaluation and reassessment as the therapy progresses.

PHASE 8: REEVALUATION

REEVALUATION AND THE ART OF TRANSITION

Phase 8 of EMDR therapy is often misunderstood, especially if a clinician's approach to EMDR is finding the ideal targeting sequence and assuming that resolving the target will be a quick fix. Although powerful generalization effects are possible in EMDR therapy, it is important to remember that EMDR therapy is much more than a technique—it is an approach to psychotherapy that honors the past, present, and future orientations of Shapiro's ultimate "three-pronged" protocol for conceptualizing EMDR therapy. With the same spirit of honoring transition in Phase 7, we also approach Phase 8, Reevaluation.

Reevaluation is the art of checking back in and planning the next moves in EMDR therapy. Major facets of Phase 8 include working with the skill of future template and reevaluating Phase 1, Client History, to determine if any other memories initially uncovered will need reprocessing. Because there is a great potential for generalization effects happening in EMDR therapy, it is possible that not every memory identified in Client History will need to be targeted. Yet in certain special circumstances and with clients who are not able to generalize or reason abstractly, more targets may need to be set up for a client to reach desired goals. Other issues may have surfaced, either in the client's life or in the course of reprocessing other targets. Residual disturbance may require therapeutic attention using the EMDR approach. For clients with meditation or other holistic practices (e.g., yoga, dance, other movement experiences, body or energy work), what emerges during the practices themselves can highlight new terrain that may need to be targeted and reprocessed. Clients with dedicated meditation or yoga practices can elect to go on regular retreats of any length from half a day to two weeks. Regardless of the length, there is ample space available in the experience for new insights, issues, and targets to emerge.

A useful way to approach Phase 8, Reevaluation, is for the clinician and client to collaboratively ask, "Where do we go next?" After every completed target, you are encouraged to ask this question with mindful intent. Sometimes clinicians must ask this question in the middle of targets that do not seem to be moving in the best possible way with respect to the goals clients have identified for treatment. The importance of regarding EMDR as an approach to psychotherapy, instead of just as a technique, is to always keep the client and the client's goals in the driver's seat of the therapeutic process. Too many EMDR clinicians can be overzealous about what they would like to see EMDR do, instead of letting the client's goals and preferences lead. Perhaps you began a targeting sequence that made sense as a starting place in Phase 1, Client History, yet proved too overwhelming for a client to handle initially. In an opposite scenario, maybe you discover that the target unearthed in Client History is not sufficiently charged when you arrive at Phase 3, Assessment. As client and clinician, you may have to go back to the proverbial drawing board to determine a target. Targeting sequences are the essential threads in the tapestry of EMDR therapy; they are the medium in which we work to bring about a client's desired treatment effect. Like in any quality art-making process, sometimes what the textbook tells you to do is not what optimally translates, so you must begin again. Reevaluate. Fortunately, there is a whole phase in EMDR therapy that allows for this process.

Tracking Targets

It is advisable to keep track, in some organized way, of targets and the future templates on which they work with clients. Some clients' presenting issues will require fewer targeting sequences than others; with more complicated clients, trial and error may be involved. Working with client feedback at the client's level of distress tolerance in handling the various targets, especially in the scope of what is going on in their life, is vital. Keeping clients' goals in the scope of their overall treatment plan (see Chapter 5) also helps you to conduct reevaluation in as mindful a way as possible. Exhibit 9.2 illustrates how to track targeting sequences used in EMDR therapy (a blank copy appears in the Appendix for your use); this tool can assist you in reevaluation. New and seasoned EMDR therapists alike can find working with multiple targets over the course of treatment confusing, particularly when complex clients present for services. Staying organized can help you navigate through the confusion.

EXHIBIT 9.2 Simple Targeting Sequence List for Clinical Tracking

Sample Client Sandy (See Chapter 5)

TARGET SET-UP (PHASES 3–7)	OUTCOME/PLAN
1. I am not in control: targeted memory of elementary school bullying.	Completed 2/2/16
2. I am in control of my responses: future template on situations that can trigger at work.	Completed 2/9/16
3. I cannot handle it: targeted memory of cousin's death when client was 13.	Started 2/9/16 Completed 3/1/16
4. I am capable of dealing with emotion: future template connected to several possible relationship scenarios and client's fear of vulnerability.	Started 3/1/2016 Completed 3/8/2016
4. I have to be perfect: targeted memory of mother's first inappropriate disclosure about her own unhappiness in her marriage.	Started 3/15/2016
	Incomplete target; client chose to put processing on pause while his mother is recovering from a surgery. Asked to revisit resources for a few sessions, concerned with ability to handle what might come up working on this material during her illness.
5. I am not safe in this world: targeted memory of bullying by a stranger at age 8 due to stranger's perception of sexual orientation. Future template completed related to national climate and threat of LGBT rights being threatened.	Completed 4/8/2016
	Client reports feeling better about revisiting perfectionism target with mother.

The Importance of Future Templates

The future template is one of the most powerful, yet often most overlooked, tools in the EMDR therapy approach. Many training programs gloss over future templates as an afterthought, if they mention them at all. Although Shapiro writes eloquently about future templates in her own text, some EMDR therapists have never used a future template with clients. Many EMDR therapists interpret Shapiro's instructions to mean that future templates should only be used at the end of treatment after every relevant target has been processed. Although using future templates as part of a final reevaluation process prior to termination is a sound strategy, Shapiro's description of the future template can be interpreted as an invitation to use it throughout the treatment process. Guiding a client through a future template after each completed target allows for more natural flow and organic clinical decision making in the reevaluation process.

Per EMDRIA's guidelines for clinical flexibility, it is possible to set up a targeting sequence in the future tense if clinically warranted. This modification is different from what is meant by a future template. Future templates are to be used only after a memory or incident has been fully processed and the positive cognition has been installed. The future template is a tool that helps us to further install the positive cognition into the future tense of the three-pronged protocol, allowing for maximum crystallization of treatment benefit. Sometimes, the future template process reveals new and unexpected material that may be processed through to resolution in the future template itself. In other situations, the material that keeps a client from holding the positive cognition as a completely true statement in the future tense reveals what target or series of targets will need to be explored next.

Consider the case of Lara, a biracial lesbian in her early 30s who worked at a clinic. In her first experience with targeting a traumatic memory in EMDR therapy, she elected to work first on her self-esteem issues. The negative cognition of "I'm not good enough" was targeted in the protocol connected to an early memory of being criticized publicly by her father. After successful processing of the touchstone memory, the therapist moved on to future template work by challenging Lara to identify a scenario that would be likely to transpire in her life in upcoming weeks. One of Lara's presenting concerns related to not being appropriately assertive at work. For the future template, Lara chose a common scenario—needing to advocate for herself and her team to the owner of the clinic, an individual she described as emotionally detached and misogynistic. In going through the future template, Lara's VoC of "I am good enough" decreased to a 5 initially and was not able to return to any higher than 6. In exploring what kept the VoC from being a 7 again in the future state, Lara surmised that safety issues prevented the VoC from holding completely. Through a conversation that assisted with the reevaluation process, Lara explained that because of her sexuality, she never felt safe in her community. Furthermore, her sense of not believing she is safe was compounded by many other microaggressions, related to her race and her gender, that she experienced throughout her life.

EMDR therapists are generally familiar with Shapiro's three main categories of responsibility, safety, and choice to describe negative cognitions related to traumatic experience. Some EMDR clinicians strictly interpret the list's order to mean responsibility cognitions must be cleared first, followed by safety and, then, power. We have discovered that the complicated nature of how trauma manifests requires more fluidity in how we move through cognitions and issues to target; the relationships between the cognition categories often vary from client to client. As in Lara's case, using the future template offered an organic way to conceptualize where to go next in her work. With Lara, approaching "I am not safe" as what Levis and Siniego (2016) describe as an oppressive cognition revealed several potential touchstone memories connected to early discrimination and feeling different from her peers. By targeting one specific touchstone memory about being excluded at age 8 from a school friend's party, Lara was able to transform "I am not safe" to "I can assure for my own safety." In working with safety, especially with vulnerable populations, it is important to consider that "I am safe" as a global statement may not feel like a realistic cognition to embrace. As with many aspects of EMDR therapy, it is important to let clients lead with language and ideas that feel most organic for them. Of course, EMDR therapists are there to facilitate and do some gentle steering through the protocol, if needed; fundamentally, the mindful EMDR therapist always remembers that the client is in control of the journey.

EMDR Therapy Case Conceptualization and Treatment-Plan Review

If you spent any time working in the trenches of community mental health or in a hospital-based treatment setting, you may associate the process of filling out treatment plans and conducting regular treatment-plan reviews as needless bureaucratic paperwork. Learning in graduate internship how to write treatment plans and regularly review them may be the source of some of your stressful memories. Challenge yourself to reframe the treatment-planning process as an exercise in EMDR therapy case conceptualization. If you have moved into more of a private-practice setting and your treatment-planning strategies have gotten lax, consider how revisiting the practice of treatment planning and treatment-plan review can help you mindfully regard the wholeness of EMDR therapy.

Chapter 5 contains a sample treatment plan that can be used in EMDR therapy. This plan is written in a common language that many of you recognize from agency or hospital-based work. This plan is the thread that connects EMDR Phase 1 to EMDR Phase 8, with the time it takes to move through that thread, the other phases, differing from client to client. Although the sample treatment plan looks complete, regard it as a fluid document. In the first pass through Phase 1, the plan may appear rudimentary and exploratory. By the time you and a client arrive for the first time at Phase 8, additions and omissions may be necessary and shifts in how targets and futures templates will be approached may need to be noted.

An important lesson from 12-step programs is that an individual can continue to work the steps repeatedly. A person in recovery is not "done" just because they have reached step 12. Long-term meditators, yogis, and contemplative mystics embrace much of the same philosophy: we can always begin again, we can always return to practicing from a beginner's mind. You can approach EMDR therapy similarly—one pass through the phases is generally not sufficient with most clients. Every time you arrive at Phase 8, the process requires us to circle back to Phase 1. Yes, in EMDR therapy clinicians hope that clients will be able to successfully terminate therapy at some point following their final reevaluation of targets and meeting of their identified goals and objectives for a specific treatment episode. But the reality is that life will continue to happen, and life is suffering. Suffering is born of craving, clinging, and aversion that often arise below the level of conscious awareness from our survival instincts, triggered in our clients by adverse life experiences. Suffering can be ended, so the Buddha suggested, by essentially replacing these survival-driven reactions with wisdom, ethical living, and mindfulness. Other teachers have suggested replacing the word "end" in relation to suffering with "transform" (Batchelor & Halifax, 2015). Whether a transformation or a cessation, EMDR therapy as an approach, when applied mindfully, increases exponentially the possibility of a more adaptive life, free of maladaptively stored memories running the show. We no longer crave, cling, or are averse to that which we experience. Rather, we meet it mindfully, adaptively.

With that perspective in mind, new traumatic experiences may necessitate clients returning for other work, or the realities of life may unearth other layers to address. You, as a therapist, have a right to establish whatever policies you may choose around termination and allowing for further contact. Remain open-minded to the complex nature of life and embrace how EMDR therapy as an approach, coupled with the wisdom of mindfulness practice, can be enlisted at any time to engage the healing process that we all so richly deserve.

TYING IT ALL TOGETHER

One might consider it poetically elegant that the eight phases of EMDR therapy conclude with Closure and Reevaluation. However, these two phases often do not occur during the same session. Closure provides an ending to a dedicated period of reprocessing and establishes the safety necessary to go back into the world. Reevaluation often occurs the next time we meet with the client, at an entire new session, usually in a different week. The reprocessing that continues between sessions can intimately connect these two phases. If clinicians teach mindfulness while also providing EMDR therapy, our clients will have the potential to move throughout their day-to-day existence more mindfully, safely, grounded, and connected. Therapy is not just an event that takes place in an office. EMDR therapists hope that clients are able to move into their lives more adaptively on an ongoing basis, and are able to notice the changes when they are out and about in their lives.

Reevaluation is another way of framing the life mindfully lived. We, clients and clinicians alike, continue to notice and to build wisdom. Then, we set intention based on our reevaluation of our EMDR therapy and our day-to-day lives. Our process in the office comes to mirror our lives moving through the world. Closure becomes not an ending, but the beginning of another phase of growth and change. Reevaluation takes into account all that we have learned to help make the next choices in service of the recovery of our clients. Mindfulness moves it all along, helping therapist and client to enter the flow of life more skillfully, more adaptively, and more capable of loving kindness and compassion for self and others. This leads to a greater sense of equanimity, that balance under any condition that allows for peace of mind, peace in relationship, and peace with ourselves.

QUESTIONS FOR REFLECTION AND PERSONAL PRACTICE

- What does it mean to you to "honor transition"?

- In what areas of your life have you experienced the importance of proper closure of an experience and/or effective use of transition?

- How can or how does your mindfulness practice better assist you in working with the art of transition and closure?

- In the spirit of learning from your mistakes, what is an experience you have had in EMDR therapy with not adequately closing a session? In light of the knowledge gained in this book and through your mindful practices, how would you have proceeded differently?

- What does it mean for you, on a personal level, to reevaluate?

REFERENCES

Batchelor, S., & Halifax, J. (Speakers). (2015, March 27). *The second great vow (Being completely human part 6)* [Audio Podcast]. Retrieved from https://www.upaya.org/2015/04/stephen-batchelor-and-joan-halifax-the-second-great-vow-being-completely-human-part-6/

Levis, R. V., & Siniego, L. B. (2016). An integrative framework for EMDR therapy as an anti-oppression endeavor. In M. I. Nickerson (Ed.), *Cultural competence and healing culturally based trauma with EMDR therapy: Innovative strategies and protocols* (pp. 79–96). New York, NY: Springer Publishing.

Marich, J. (2010). EMDR in addiction continuing care: A phenomenological study of women in early recovery. *Psychology of Addictive Behaviors, 24*(3), 498–507.

Shapiro, F. (2001). *Eye movement desensitization and reprocessing: Basic principles, protocols, and procedures* (2nd ed.). New York, NY: Guilford Press.

10

Enhancing Your Efficacy as a Therapist: Developing Your Own Mindfulness Practice and Doing Your Own Trauma Work

"May you live in interesting times."

In 1966, Robert F. Kennedy referenced this translation of a saying that was often misunderstood as a blessing when, in fact, it was meant as a curse. Kennedy added that his times were full of "great danger and uncertainty, but they are . . . also more open to the creative energy of men than any other time in history." By this definition, we live today—on a global level and in the world of psychotherapy—in extremely interesting times. From a mindfulness perspective, this reality is both a blessing and a curse. In the midst of difficulty and tragedy, we can all find healing of the highest order. Out of the ancient wisdom of mindfulness, the active and applied wisdom of many global cultures of holistic healing, and the revolutionary discoveries in Western psychotherapy, trauma-focused care is born. As clinicians and as human beings, we can meet these interesting times with a formula that moves beyond simple surviving. Perhaps we, clinicians and clients alike, will be able to thrive.

In this concluding chapter, the challenge is for readers to embrace humankind's innate ability to flourish. For EMDR therapists specifically, consider that without mindfulness practices, EMDR therapy may in fact be incomplete, as is our ability to be ambassadors for this call to thrive. To make this case, this chapter includes sharing from several EMDR therapists who are discovering the beautiful fusion of EMDR therapy and mindfulness practice as a way of life. The experiences of other leaders in the field are also cited, furthering the contention that mindfulness practice enhances professional competence. Other topics explored in this chapter include insights for developing practices under the guidance of teachers and supporting other therapists in their quest to develop as trauma-focused practitioners. The book concludes with a revolutionary call to action, defining how we, as clinicians, can better care for ourselves and the people we serve. This challenge contains a blueprint for thriving in action, and for the great circle of healing to continue in its marvelous splendor.

MINDFULNESS AND EMDR THERAPY: INTIMATELY CONNECTED

Ever since Francine Shapiro's walk in the park, there has been a willingness on her part and a great desire in the EMDR community to see how this therapy could be worked with, revised, improved, and practiced as a complete approach to psychotherapy. This evolution is manifest at any EMDRIA conference, where new protocols for specific populations are regularly introduced, innovative revisions to the standard eight-phase protocol are given voice, integrative strategies with other psychotherapy traditions are discussed, and advances in the visioning and implementation of treatment are proposed and researched. Major turning points over the last three decades proved to be important growth opportunities in the evolution of EMDR therapy. One such turning point was mentioned in Chapter 6, when, in 2005, Dworkin described Leeds and Korn's Resource Development and Installation (RDI) as the missing piece of the standard protocol. Through treatment failures, Leeds and others found a pathway to help most anyone become capable of reprocessing. This may not have been the last of the advances in the reimagining of the eight-phase protocol and the adaptive information processing model, but it certainly represented a sea change.

EMDR therapists now find themselves on the precipice of a similar opportunity. Many changes in EMDR therapy over the decades can be described as implicit aspects of the therapy becoming explicit. New protocols are developed, or attachment theory and other critical elements are integrated into our case conceptualization and delivery of treatment. With these changes, EMDR therapists are not so much adding to what we do. Rather, we are honoring the diversity of issues, needs, and goals of our clients and bringing in new knowledge to collaborate on strategies and solutions with those who come to us for help. These advances, whether they come in the form of integrative models, new resourcing opportunities, alternative protocols, or revised case-conceptualization strategies, all point toward our continued commitment as a community to finding our way to end suffering for as many people as we possibly can.

The true nature of this opportunity was made clear in two of Shapiro's assertions in 2014. First, in a letter to the EMDRIA membership, Shapiro requested that EMDR therapists should start referring to EMDR as "EMDR therapy." This simple yet powerful change suggests to our profession and to the general public that EMDR therapy is a complete approach to psychotherapeutic care. Second, "small-t traumas" are now referred to as "adverse life experiences" (Shapiro, 2014), a term that references the dilemma of being a human being, rather than focusing only on the highly traumatic experiences outside the realm of day-to-day experience. The implication is that EMDR therapy can help people with trauma-driven complaints other than PTSD, including many of the diagnoses in the DSM-5 as well as problems in daily living that clinicians and clients choose not to label with a diagnosis. Therefore, EMDR therapy now can serve as a primary modality or even a theoretical orientation for clinicians. Shapiro's commitment (and the commitment from those who followed with research) to helping us all find out that EMDR therapy is an evidence-based treatment for PTSD is opening a world in which we can treat so many of our clients with this powerful therapy for a wide variety of concerns.

All of this leads us back to mindfulness and its role in EMDR therapy. EMDR is already conceptualized by many as a mindfulness-based therapy. This quality of mindfulness needs to be cultivated in the therapist as a best practice for both clinician self-care and client care, while mindfulness developed in the client insures a greater possibility of success through each of the eight phases of Shapiro's protocol. Some of these mindfulness aspects are explicit in Shapiro's original text as well as in the standard protocol and AIP model, and many are implicit. Our larger vision is that clinicians will appreciate the link between EMDR therapy and mindfulness as front and center, once and for all. EMDR therapy, artfully delivered by a mindfulness-informed therapist to a mindfulness-trained client, can be the gold standard going forward. All the other theoretical orientations brought to the table by EMDR therapists and trainers, any and all alternative protocols, and, most importantly, the standard eight-phase protocol guided by the AIP model, all become that much more effective when applied with mindful intention and mindful awareness.

This book showcases the presence of mindfulness throughout the standard protocol and in the language of EMDR therapy. Phase 1 begins to teach the client a new way of looking at and experiencing trauma and adverse life experiences. As opposed to giving in to stories they have told themselves over and again, clients are encouraged to simply notice a moment in time—a moment accompanied by suffering. Clinicians generally know beforehand how we will be able to use this information. When Phase 1 is mindfully applied, the client begins to develop that same experiential knowledge, and soon, becomes a collaborator in their care. Much like the overall role of mindfulness in EMDR therapy, our psychoeducation of the client is both explicit and implicit. Clinicians help the client to understand what we know of the theoretical underpinnings, the research, the brain science, and the history of EMDR therapy, while also providing the in vivo skill-building of *noticing*, rather than *ruminating*.

In Phase 2, the skills of mindfulness practice can be overtly applied. The guided visualizations of Calm Safe Place, Light Stream, and the Container are all examples of building the skill of concentration to facilitate a greater state of mindfulness. In the tradition of Buddhist mindfulness, there are three factors of the path of mindfulness that are dedicated specifically to the practice of meditation: Effort, Mindfulness, and Concentration. In Phase 2, EMDR therapists can still utilize the original techniques proposed by Shapiro rooted in guided visualization. We can, however, bolster their healing potential, helping clients identify, reengage, develop, and install mindfulness-based internal and external resources that will liberate them on their unique journey. We need to be clearly client-centered in this aspect. We need to discover the skills and resources with which your individual clients will make the effort to engage. You will find that the more you honor clients as the experts on themselves and their own lives, the greater the possible effort they will invest. Mindfulness, that ability to maintain nonjudgmental awareness of the present moment, can be developed with classical Buddhist mindfulness, creative mindfulness, DBT skills, yoga, and a variety of other modalities. Furthermore, concentration is similarly going to be developed through these practices, which will only increase the capacity for mindful noticing of the present moment. We are teaching our clients not only how to concentrate; more significantly, we are teaching them how to concentrate on the right things, in the right way, to bring them to health.

Phases, 3 through 6, the reprocessing phases, are where mindful skill building, experiential knowledge development, and gathering of self-knowledge launch into dynamic use. If Phases 1 and 2 have been delivered and experienced with mindfulness, our accessing of the target and its related beliefs, emotions, level of disturbance, and body sensations will go more smoothly and more quickly. The client will be more likely to apply concentration at each step in the targeting process and mindfully move on to the next aspect of the experience. Each item builds on the one before it, so that when Desensitization commences in Phase 4 there is maximum activation, facilitated in a large part by mindfulness and concentration. The language of the Desensitization phase is quite clear about the mindfulness that is inherent in this work: "Go with that." "Just notice." "What are you noticing now?" The desensitization and reprocessing of this material continues to move through our own mindful attention to the verbal and somatic cues from the client, and through the direct application of mindfulness skills on the part of the client. As clinicians, our mindfulness allows for a continuing commitment to staying out of the way as much as possible, and making sure any interweaves mimic organic reprocessing.

This flow can enhance a clinician's larger commitment to allowing the client's mind, body, and spirit to do their own healing. New pathways are created, disturbances are reduced, those aspects of the memory that are no longer useful fall away, and the relationship to the memory is changed. In keeping with the original teachings in Buddhist psychology, suffering is reduced not through a decrease of the pain of life; rather, it happens through a change in our relationship to the pain, the joy, the boredom—all of life experience. Phases 3 and 4 facilitate this reduction or ending of suffering related to a particular memory, and sometimes simultaneously for associated memories. Phase 5 allows clients, now hopefully free of the prison created by the maladaptively stored memory, to focus their concentration and mindfulness upon the installation of a positive belief that can now propel their motivation forward. A Subjective Units of Despair (SUDs) of 0 and a Validity of Cognition (VoC) of 7, and the process moves into Phase 6, Body Scan, to see if the work is indeed complete. In this concluding phase of reprocessing, we invite clients to explore the body once again to determine if we have reprocessed completely.

Another phase where mindfulness has perhaps been most practiced throughout the history of EMDR therapy is in Phase 7, Closure. So much of the closure process is about safety; specifically, inviting the mindful noticing of present reality and the world that the client is returning to after the session. When clients are encouraged to activate their difficult material and reprocess, they can feel disoriented once that process comes to a close. Even completing a target and the monumental relief it can bring can be accompanied by confusion or distractedness. Much like EMDR therapists practice during the resource identification and building stage, we identify and utilize those resources that will help the client to make the transition out of the office. Regardless of a complete or incomplete target, there is indeed a transition, and we alert the client at the end of each session when we remind them that reprocessing may continue outside the office. Sometimes these will be direct applications of mindfulness, such as grounding or meditation. Other times, clinicians may use other interventions applied with the spirit and practice of mindfulness. Our role continues to be staying out of the way as much as possible. At the same time, we are that much more mindful as therapists of the level of containment and holding necessary for each client after each session to make that transition safe and successful.

The mindful approach continues through to the conclusion of the standard protocol, Phase 8, Reevaluation. EMDR therapy is more of a mindful wheel of healing than a road with a destination. Consider the similarities to the 12-step community's teaching that the steps ought to be taken over and again as opposed to being a finite exercise. The Buddha prescribed an Eightfold Path where, at the end, individuals are brought back to the first factor of wisdom and, in a sense, begin again. These all represent healing circles that human beings can keep around us as part of our experience and protection for a lifetime. At the same time, these healing circles—specifically the eight phases of EMDR therapy—are a treatment with a beginning, middle, and end. The end of one client's therapy will include a final Phase 8, a reevaluation of all targets with the goal of leaving nothing behind. In the session-to-session context, mindfulness guides a successful Phase 8. On the therapist's side, we must be practicing mindfulness to maintain our ability to understand the ongoing process that the client experiences, even between sessions. For clients, mindfulness will help them maintain their ability to stay grounded between sessions, allow them to witness the continuing reprocessing, and let them mimic the flow of reprocessing because they are in the flow of life, rather than fighting with demons blindly or through rumination.

MINDFULNESS: A WAY OF LIFE

These links to mindfulness within the protocol can be illuminated by your ongoing experience with mindfulness practice. The ebb and flow of your life may get in the way of the most consistent practice possible. Consider how the lessons you may have learned as an EMDR therapist to "stay out of the way" as much as possible can help you in our own journey. Allow the qualities of nonjudgment and self-compassion to be cultivated in your mindfulness practice. Do not let the quest to "do it right" become one more thing to stress you out. Consistency is more important than the hours spent on practicing mindfulness; quality trumps quantity. A consistent attending to mindfulness is what is important, regardless of the wisdom and modalities used to get there. It is most important to find the types of practice that can be sustained, even if a little at a time.

Please practice patience with yourself if this process does not happen for you instantly. Consider the journey of EMDR therapist Thomas Zimmerman. Tom is a case study in not taking to mindful, embodied practices naturally, and he arrived at EMDR therapy as a skeptic. When Tom was in graduate school, he was a self-professed walking advertisement for cognitive behavioral therapy. Now, a Certified EMDR Therapist and training facilitator with a successful holistic practice, Tom describes the early stages of his journey as a clinician in training and what made embodiment so scary:

Breathing and noticing were highly triggering for me in the beginning in ways that had little to do with either breathing or noticing my breath. They were wrapped up with performance anxiety. They were wrapped up in other "inside" stuff. Like my clients, they "didn't work for me" for a long time and I didn't want to hear it. Then, I dipped my toe in. I dipped my toe in again. I feel like I'm up to my waist now, and the temperature feels just fine. Breathing as a resource clicked in for me two years ago because it had to. My past and present were colliding at places where there were once carefully constructed overpasses. My anxiety skyrocketed and I had difficulty thinking or rationalizing my way out. Once I incorporated deep breathing into my daily life, it was much easier to engage clients with it. Finding my own way into breathing taught me a lot about the obstacles and some ways around them. Listening very closely to clients taught me even more about the obstacles and ways around them.

Tom writes a very popular blog, *Go With That,* on his adventures as an EMDR therapist. Visit his site (https://gowiththat.wordpress.com) to learn more about his journey toward discovering a life mindfully lived and an EMDR therapy mindfully practiced.

Irene Rodriguez, a Certified EMDR Therapist originally from Puerto Rico who now practices in Florida, describes how her mindfulness practice translates into her clinical practice:

As a clinician, the mindfulness attitudes of nonstriving and acceptance have been a great impact in my practice because it helps me to reduce anxiety regarding expecting any results from the therapy session. I've been encouraging my clients to be aware of their breathing, their body sensations, and practicing noticing without judgment during the therapy sessions. I also encourage them to create a space between their thoughts and their body sensations. Almost in every session, I encourage them to stop fighting their symptoms and to accept whatever is happening. Then I teach them that once we have accepted whatever is going on, we can move on by listening and paying attention to their body needs. As a therapist practicing the attitudes of mindfulness while doing EMDR therapy sessions, I cultivate attention and awareness of my client and their therapy process. Also, it has helped me to be comfortable at times of stillness, silence, and embrace client's abreactions. I believe that I'm a better clinician every time that I'm aware of my thoughts, feelings, and sensations. With that awareness I'm able to be compassionate toward myself and my clients.

The mindfulness practices suggested in Chapter 3 cover a wide swath of the territory that one can use as both a starting point for a dedicated mindfulness practice and as guides to sustain this practice. There are many variations on the 2,600-year-old wisdom of Buddhist mindfulness, but all of them return to what is pertinent for all EMDR therapists: the practices of mindfulness of body, feelings, thoughts, and dharmas (or conceptual thought) all promote the development of concentration, thus developing a greater ability to enter states of mindfulness. The correct effort placed toward these practices enables it to have energy and be sustainable. More wisdom is generated through the practice, and we can set more skillful and harmless intentions. Then, we can practice in the world through our speech, our actions, and our livelihood as therapists (Dansiger, 2016). As covered throughout this book, mindfulness allows us to see how staying out of the way as much as possible helps empower our clients and give them the space to heal. Clinicians can also use our own mindfulness practice to better guide our clients when that is necessary. We will better intuit when to step in as processing needs to be unblocked or safety needs to be established or reestablished. Mindfulness is not just about meditation. It becomes an integral aspect of our humanity, a way of being and acting in the world. That is the mindfulness at the heart and soul of this book: mindfulness as a way of life.

Notice how the fruits of mindfulness practice can show up in your life as marvelous gifts. A regular day at the office can easily turn into a maelstrom of stressors. In addition to dealing with a client crisis on a day when you are hoping to catch up on a mountain of unanswered email, suddenly your partner may text you to announce that the water damage in the bathroom requires that the shower and floor be replaced. However these stresses can show up in your body, you can learn to take refuge in the simplicity of a deep breath . . . or three. Maybe that refuge presents itself in the form of a simple, improvisational dance, series of yoga poses, or a five-minute return to Beginner's Mind, accessed right there in the office. Although many of us are programmed by modern American culture and the necessity to multitask and to push through, the ultimate self-care you can gift yourself is to take those moments to breathe. In doing so, you will find that you can respond to stress instead of react to stress. Sometimes the waves of life have even graver implications than a bad day at the office. Maybe the sociopolitical climate of the modern world has rocked you in a profound way. Perhaps your suffering has come in the form of death, loss, or unexpected transition.

In some way as a human being, you have encountered adverse life experiences. Our larger global family struggles to cope with the reality of suffering on a daily basis, calling attention to the wider context. Mindfulness practices, contrary to what some savvy marketing would have us believe, are not a quick fix or an easy cure. They are, however, part of the solution. When applied consistently, you may begin to see small transformations in your life that over time can manifest as huge, life-changing shifts in consciousness. The helping professions are becoming increasingly more receptive to this wisdom. While mindful practice is not a panacea, mindfulness is definitely one of the very best practices for facilitating healthy living. When embedded within other best practices, mindfulness can provide, enhance, and promote that same effect for that with which it is joined.

There are several high-profile examples of blending mindfulness with other wisdom practices and therapeutic interventions. Jon Kabat-Zinn is often credited with introducing mindfulness to the clinical world with Mindfulness-Based Stress Reduction (MBSR). While serving as faculty at the University of Massachusetts Medical School, he noticed that helping chronic pain patients change their relationship to their pain through mindfulness could alleviate their pain (Kabat-Zinn, 2003). This is an application of classical Buddhist mindfulness to a clinical dilemma, the honoring of the second noble truth of the Buddha that the cause of suffering is not caused by that stimulus that creates the pain, but instead from our craving for the pain to go away and our aversion to the pain. His findings have led to many other therapies and techniques that are mindfulness-based or mindfulness-informed, including solutions for depression, anxiety, and a host of other difficulties. Marsha Linehan saw that traditional cognitive behavioral therapy (CBT) techniques did not reach clients with borderline personality disorder; in fact, it would often exacerbate the problem. She drew on her own Zen Buddhist training to transform CBT and create dialectal behavioral therapy, essentially a mindfulness-training program embedded within the CBT framework (Linehan, 1993). Her therapy design kept in mind that clients with personality disorders could be the most difficult and long-term clients, whose therapy would need to be done as a team and whose members would need to develop their own mindfulness skills. She also made it clear how important it is that we go into the pain and through the pain, not try to escape it. Mark Epstein has written several books where he has applied his Buddhist training that preceded his medical school experience to make a call for a more mindful approach to psychiatry. His *Thoughts Without a Thinker* (2013) and *Psychotherapy Without a Self* (2008) mirror Shapiro's call to stay out of the way as much as possible. Dan Siegel spends a great deal of time writing and speaking on the ongoing developments in brain science that point toward the efficacy of mindfulness. His commitment to linking the science and practice of mindfulness is taken further at UCLA, where he is based at the Semel Institute. There, mindfulness training is developed, provided, and researched from academic, theoretical, and practical perspectives.

There is also a growing body of evidence to suggest that clinicians who practice mindfulness and related practices such as yoga are not only healthier, they are more effective clinicians because of their practice (Christopher et al., 2011; Davis & Hayes, 2011; Greason & Cashwell, 2009; Maris, 2009; Newsome, Waldo, & Gruszka, 2012; Schuer, Christopher, & Christopher, 2008; Tarrasch, 2014). An informal review of the literature (originally taken on to provide data for a state licensing board) shows clearly that "mindful self-care" programs are becoming an important model in clinician continuing education. Several key findings to note:

- Promoting mindfulness in psychotherapists-in-training could positively influence the therapeutic course and treatment results in patients (randomized, double-blind controlled study; Grepmair et al., 2007).

- Health care professionals participating in a mindfulness-based stress reduction program were able to more fully identify their own themes of perfectionism, the automaticity of "other focus," and their tendencies to always enter "fixer" mode; this recognition led to numerous changes along personal and professional domains (grounded theory; Irving et al., 2014); a similar study that exclusively studied nurses yielded similar findings (Frisvold, Lindquist, & McAlpine, 2012).

- In an extensive mixed-methods research study with working psychotherapists from a variety of theoretical backgrounds, Keane (2013) concluded that personal mindfulness practice can enhance key therapist abilities (e.g., attention) and qualities (e.g., empathy) that have a positive influence on therapeutic training.

- Dr. Jennifer Sharp, a dancing mindfulness facilitator and faculty member at Northern Kentucky University, along with her colleague Dr. Susannah Coaston, presented preliminary research at the American Association of Creativity in Counseling's 2016 annual conference on the positive impact of dancing mindfulness practice on personal and professional well-being. They are currently preparing this research, investigating close to 100 clinicians and other wellness professionals who practice dancing mindfulness, for publication.

FINDING YOUR TEACHERS AND YOUR COMMUNITY

With growing belief in the integration of mindfulness and EMDR therapy, there is increased interest in honoring and encouraging the growth of a supportive community. Both authors give a great deal of credit to their own teachers and those alongside whom they have practiced mindfulness in community over the years. In the Zen tradition, monks would wander from temple to temple seeking a teacher, and traditionally would sit outside the gate for days waiting for the opportunity to work with a particular teacher.

In the early Buddhist teachings all the way through to the 21st century, mindfulness seekers have been encouraged to find teachers who speak directly to them. There are many different flavors of teaching, representing all stages of history and all kinds of cultural contexts. At this time, it might seem, like so much in our social media and tech-driven world, that there are way too many choices and it all becomes overwhelming. Many religious historians and spiritualists speak of all paths leading to one. And in this case, if one seeks within the framework of Buddhist mindfulness and its associated mindfulness-based practices, where the practice leads one into and through the pain rather than escaping, you will be able to find the teacher or teachers who speak to you. This is about your own practice, your own mindfulness journey, and not about our learning mindfulness skills sets to deliver to others. Again, you do not have to live in a monastery for a year or become a mindfulness teacher yourself in any context outside of your clinical office. Start by working on the suggestions in this book and other wise guidance you receive from mindful mentors to bring about healing for yourself, and then for others, through the mindful application of EMDR therapy. In that process, you can improve your own quality of life by living mindfully, both professionally and personally.

The mindfulness equivalent of bibliotherapy, including print, digital, and audiobook, provides a voice for teachers. In these forms, such teachers in the Buddhist tradition as Kabat-Zinn, Jack Kornfield, Sharon Salzberg, Joseph Goldstein, Ajahn Chah, Tara Brach, Noah Levine, and Thich Nhat Hanh, and the historical Buddha primarily as translated by Bhikkhu Bodhi, are easily accessed by the public. While you may recognize those names as the rock stars of contemporary Buddhist teaching, please do not feel that your teacher must be a "big name" to provide you with wise guidance. Terry Fralich, a lawyer-turned-clinician and the author of two user-friendly books on mindfulness practice, has a special gift for teaching clinicians and the lay public. While not necessarily a media-grabbing name in Buddhist discourse, Fralich beautifully conveys the wisdom received during more than 30 years of traveling with the Dalai Lama. Christine Valters Paintner, an expressive-arts educator and author of 10 books, is an excellent teacher of mindfulness within a Christian framework. Paintner is a lay Benedictine abbess and yoga teacher who draws from a variety of global traditions in her teaching, which is geared toward the lay public. Her work may be a good starting point if you are a Christian who is hesitant to work with mindfulness because of its roots in Eastern practice. Christine has a lovely way of demonstrating, with real-world candor, how the meditation traditions in our human history have more similarities than differences.

While some classical Buddhist practitioners profess to follow one teacher in their practice, you may consider adopting what EMDR therapist and Certified DBT Therapist Rachel Weaver calls a "tapas" approach to spiritual learning. Like the small plates in the Spanish tradition that can offer a full meal of variety and flavor, consider how the various teachers who cross your path can contribute to your nourishment. You may find yourself reading Sharon Salzberg, sitting with a local meditation teacher at a nearby yoga studio, and going to a national conference in your field to take in a presentation on mindfulness—all in the same week. All avenues provide valid teaching. Your clients, if you let them, can be your greatest teachers. So can your successes—and, more importantly, your failures, the cases you wish you could have handled differently. The most difficult people in your life, the figures on the international stage who challenge the way you see the world—how has learning to respond to them instead of react to them helped you to live a more mindful life? Everyone who crosses our path is a potential teacher. Are you willing to embrace the wisdom from each teacher?

In addition to our development as mindful therapists, we can also grow as trauma-informed practitioners by studying with different teachers and engaging with a community. This book challenges us to move from a trauma-informed mindset to a bolder embrace of trauma-focused care. There are several ways to continue our growth and commitment as we make this shift. Seek continuing education and consultation in EMDR therapy, especially to receive further teaching on populations and issues in which you specialize. Clinicians become more trauma-informed in our practice through learning and manifesting best practices as they pertain to the specific clients we serve.

Furthering our education in general traumatology and the foundational principles of trauma care, and not just those principles specific to EMDR therapy, is also vital. As with mindfulness, there are many books to read, continuing education to absorb, and trauma-responsive modalities to learn. The work of Bessel van der Kolk, Peter Levine, Judith Herman, Stephen Porges, and many other trauma researchers and theoreticians can guide us. Workshops on the application of SAMHSA's principles of trauma-informed care can give us a basic template for moving forward. Learning either elements of or the complete practice of Somatic Experiencing®, Sensorimotor Psychotherapy®, the Trauma Resiliency Model®, *Seeking Safety*® or other trauma modalities can only enhance our work as trauma-informed and mindful EMDR therapists.

Last, and perhaps most importantly, consider the benefits of engaging in these practices within a community of supportive individuals. In classical Buddhist practice, *sangha* (a Sanskrit and Pali word) references an assembly or gathering of practitioners. Although traditionally seen as a gathering of monks, modern use of the term can extend to lay practitioners coming together for a common purpose. Many of us experience the benefit of sharing our practices in community. You can sit with groups regularly to practice classic meditation strategies, and you can extend the meaning of *sangha* in our personal practices to include alternative groupings as well. Maybe your yoga or conscious-dance community is a *sangha* for you. Any gathering that helps you to stay more centered in your own practice and draw inspiration from others who are walking a similar path is potentially beneficial to your overall personal and clinical growth.

There are many applications for extending the concept of *sangha* to our practice as trauma-focused practitioners. Many opportunities can exist for EMDR therapists to gather (e.g., study groups, consultation groups, regional networking meetings, the international conference). However, think about how you may derive particular benefit from fellowshipping with EMDR therapists who are also committed to mindfulness practices. Whether theses gatherings of like-minded EMDR practitioners happen formally (e.g., an organized meeting or training) or informally (e.g., gathering at a yoga studio or someone's home to practice a meditation and then transition into clinical discussion and personal support), there are opportunities to grow from this type of sustenance. When you have a challenging day, either clinically or personally, calling or texting members of your circle of support—people who understand both the clinical commitment to trauma-focused care and mindful self-compassion—can help you ride the wave of a particular challenge.

A CALL TO REVOLUTIONARY ACTION

How will clinicians be able to provide trauma-focused care with effectiveness and enthusiasm? With the integration of mindfulness and EMDR therapy, the path ahead is clear. How can clinicians integrate these two practices? The initial answer might be to learn some mindfulness techniques and teach them to clients, and then learn the eight-phase protocol and deliver it correctly and with mindfulness. There is, however, a deeper, more long-term, and sustainable solution. Clinicians need to find ways to take better care of ourselves so that we can take care of others. As an EMDR therapist, have you discovered some of your own healing through EMDR therapy? Many of us have realized that engaging in our own trauma work has made us more ready and able to sit with the trauma of others.

EMDR therapist Dr. Beth Shapiro offers her experience, strength, and hope about how this process worked for her:

> The decision to become trained in EMDR therapy has proven to be a wise path to follow for my practice, and for me personally. I must admit that originally I had some skepticism about this form of psychotherapy, having "grown up" in the talk-therapy world. I felt the best way to

understand EMDR would be to immerse myself in it, and this has provided me a new appreciation for this intervention. As a therapist based in humanistic practice in which the therapeutic relationship is paramount, EMDR fit right in with helping add another dimension to the ways I can holistically conceptualize client challenges and opportunities. It allows for the client's full life narrative to be considered, since the past informs the present.

This full immersion in EMDR therapy that Dr. Shapiro describes may be a necessary step to bolster your enthusiasm for offering EMDR in a mindful way. If you are trained in EMDR therapy and you find that her words about the humanistic approach and holistic conceptualization differ from your experience with the therapy, consider engaging in the client role once again. If it is available in your area, intentionally seek out an EMDR therapist who is not well-trained only in EMDR. Ask about the therapist's work with mindfulness or general approach when it comes to relationship-building and working with trauma-focused values. Make it personal. This work is personal and you deserve to be nourished by it.

Irene Rodriguez, who shared part of her mindfulness journey and its impact on her therapy practice earlier in the chapter, also openly speaks about how practicing EMDR therapy has changed the way she sees her clients:

Learning EMDR therapy has not only been a tool to help my clients to resolve trauma memories and develop more adaptive behaviors, but has transformed the way I interpret their symptoms. I have learned that we all are survivors in one way or another. I've been learning to see my clients through the lens of trauma and understanding the importance of providing them with options about how they want their therapy process to be. EMDR has taught me that the client is the expert and I'm just facilitating their healing process. I also have learned how important the silence can be; also the importance of not doing, or saying nothing, because sometimes space is all that the client needs. I believe that EMDR empowers clients by giving them tools to face their memories and experience all the body sensations within. They are the ones in control.

TYING IT ALL TOGETHER

We hope that this book helps your clients to receive a profound experience in EMDR therapy. With equal intention, we hope that therapists might find themselves less taxed, more invigorated, and able to mindfully apply the eight-phase protocol and the AIP model toward the lessening of difficulties produced by the maladaptive processing of our client's memories. Through our own trauma work and our own mindfulness practice, guided by the work of Pierre Janet and those who have interpreted him, guided by the teachings of Buddhist psychology through ancient and modern-day mindfulness teachers, and guided by the wisdom of the standard protocol and its modifications, we can provide trauma-focused care. The Buddha stated that he taught only one thing: the truth of suffering and the end of suffering. Perhaps in a way he was the first trauma-focused psychologist, providing trauma-focused care almost 2,600 years ago. Shapiro's AIP model presents a modern tool for understanding and bringing about the end of suffering. Both the ancient practice and the modern therapy present complementary methods for developing a new relationship to our pain, bringing profound transformation. When integrated with mindfulness in this way, EMDR therapy becomes complete. When combined, each enhances the other and brings hope where there was none, healing that seemed impossible, and the possibility of a new life. Francine Shapiro put it simply: The goal of EMDR therapy is to help the client live a more adaptive life. A more adaptive life is one that can be lived in the spirit and practice of *metta,* or loving kindness, toward self and others. Mindful EMDR therapy brings greater hope for the *metta* phrases to come true. In this spirit, we leave you with our wish for you, your clients and all beings . . .

May all beings be free from fear.

May all beings be healthy.

May all beings be happy.

May all beings be at ease.

QUESTIONS FOR REFLECTION AND PERSONAL PRACTICE

- What barriers do I face in fully committing to my own self-care?

- Do I recognize the importance of doing my own trauma work on a regular basis?

- What factors may keep me from addressing my own suffering with either mindfulness practice, EMDR therapy, or other trauma-focused strategies?

- What role do community and continuing study play in my personal development?

REFERENCES

Christopher, J. C., Chrisman, J., Trotter-Mathison, M., Schure, M., Dahlen, P., & Christopher, S. (2011). Perceptions of the long-term influence of mindfulness training on counselors and psychotherapists: A qualitative inquiry. *Journal of Humanistic Psychology, 51*(3), 318–349.

Dansiger, S. (2016). *Clinical dharma: A path for healers and helpers*. Los Angeles, CA: StartAgain.

Davis, D., & Hayes, J. (2011). What are the benefits of mindfulness? A practice review of psychotherapy-related research. *Psychotherapy, 48*(2), 198–208.

Epstein, M. (2008). *Psychotherapy without the self: A Buddhist perspective*. New Haven, CT: Yale University Press.

Epstein, M. (2013). *Thoughts without a thinker: Psychotherapy from a Buddhist perspective* (Rev. ed.). New York, NY: Basic Books.

Frisvold, M. H., Lindquist, R., & McAlpine, C. P. (2012). Living life in balance at midlife: Lessons learned from mindfulness. *Western Journal of Nursing Research, 34*, 265–278.

Greason, P., & Cashwell, C. (2009). Mindfulness & counseling self-efficacy: The mediating role of attention and empathy. *Counselor Education & Supervision, 49*, 2–19.

Grepmair, L., Mitterlehner, F., Loew, T., Bachler, E., Rother, W., & Nickel, M. (2007). Promoting mindfulness in psychotherapists in training influences the treatment results of their patients: A randomized, double-blind controlled study. *Psychotherapy and Psychosomatics, 76*, 332–338.

Irving, J. A., Park-Saltzman, J., Fitzpatrick, M., Dobkin, P. L., Chen, A., & Hutchinson, T. (2014). Experiences of health care professionals enrolled in mindfulness-based medical practice: A grounded theory model. *Mindfulness, 5*, 60–71.

Kabat-Zinn, J. (2003). Mindfulness-based interventions in context: Past, present, and future. *Clinical Psychology: Science and Practice, 10*(2), 144–156.

Keane, A. (2013). The influence of therapist mindfulness practice on psychotherapeutic work: A mixed-methods study. *Mindfulness, 5*, 689.

Kennedy, R. (1966, June 6). Day of affirmation address (news release version). Retrieved from https://www.jfklibrary.org/Research/Research-Aids/Ready-Reference/RFK-Speeches/Day-of-Affirmation-Address-news-release-text-version.aspx

Linehan, M. (1993). *Cognitive-behavioral treatment of borderline personality disorder*. New York, NY: Guildford Press.

Maris, J. (2009). The impact of a mind/body medicine class on the counselor training: A personal journey. *Journal of Humanistic Psychology, 49*(2), 229–235.

Newsome, S., Waldo, M., & Gruszka, C. (2012). Mindfulness group work: Preventing stress and increasing self-compassion among helping professionals in training. *Journal for Specialists in Group Work, 37*(4), 297–311.

Schuer, M., Christopher, J., & Christopher, S. (2008). Mind-body medicine and the art of self-care: Teaching mindfulness to counseling students through yoga, meditation, and qigong. *Journal of Counseling and Development, 86*(1), 47.

Shapiro, F. (2014). The role of eye movement desensitization and reprocessing (EMDR) therapy in medicine: Addressing the psychological and physical symptoms stemming from adverse life experience. *Permanente Journal, 18*(1), 71–77.

Tarrasch, R. (2014). Mindfulness meditation for graduate students in educational counseling and special education: A qualitative analysis. *Journal of Child and Family Studies, 24*(5), 1322–1333.

Appendix

EMDR Clinical Worksheet Templates

Phase 1: Client History Taking—General Functions for Success

Insights from general initial conversations, clinical intake, rapport building (you can supplement with any clinical intake forms you are asked to use in your place of employment):

Strengths, assets, recovery capital, and resources:

-
-
-
-
-

Goals for services (general or specific):

-
-
-
-
-
-

Client's general understanding of trauma and response to initial education about trauma-focused care:

Phase 1: Client History Taking—Identifying Themes, Negative Cognitions, and Potential Targets

Going through a detailed, chronological history is not vital. For many people, recounting a detailed history may be impossible until you have processed certain memories, or you may not feel ready for it right now. The imperative is to identify themes that are linked to presenting issues:

Theme 1 (Connected to Presenting Issue):

Negative Cognition:

- First floatback memory:
- Worst floatback memory:
- Most recent floatback memory:

Theme 2 (Connected to Presenting Issue):

Negative Cognition:

- First floatback memory:
- Worst floatback memory:
- Most recent floatback memory:

Theme 3 (Connected to Presenting Issue):

Negative Cognition:

- First floatback memory:
- Worst floatback memory:
- Most recent floatback memory:

NOTES: (a) Not required to fill out all three (depends on client presentation) or you may use additional pages if needed, (b) Use the negative cognitions list with instructions on the opposite page to help you if client is not able to readily identify themes and corresponding cognitions independently.

Phase 1: Client History Taking—The "Greatest Hits" List of Negative Cognitions (*continued*)

Responsibility

I should have known better.
I should have done something.
I did something wrong.
I am to blame.
I cannot be trusted.

Safety

I cannot trust myself.
I cannot trust anyone.
I am in danger.
I am not safe.
I cannot show my emotions.

Choice

I am not in control.
I have to be perfect/please everyone.
I am weak.
I am trapped.
I have no options.

Power

I cannot get what I want.
I cannot handle it/stand it.
I cannot succeed.
I cannot stand up for myself.
I cannot let it out.
I am powerless/helpless.

Value

I am a bad person/I am terrible.
I am permanently damaged.
I am defective.
I am worthless/inadequate.
I am insignificant.
I am not important.
I deserve to die.
I deserve only bad things.
I am stupid.
I do not belong.
I am different.
I am a failure.
I am ugly.
My body is ugly.
I am alone.

How to Use:

- Have your client check off any negative beliefs that he/she may still hold in the present, especially those that go along with the presenting issue he/she has chosen.

- If more than three are checked, have client go over the list again and try to rank (1, 2, 3) the "hottest" or "most charged" beliefs.

- Once identified, ask client three floatback questions and document on the corresponding worksheet:

Looking back over the course of your life, when is the **first** *time you believed . . . (e.g., I am . . .; I cannot . . .; I do not . . .)*

Looking back over the course of your life, when is the **worst** *time you believed . . .*

Looking back over the course of your life, when is the **most recent** *time you believed . . .*

Case Conceptualization and Treatment Plan

Use as many of these pages as you need throughout your engagement with the client. Part of Phase 8, Reevaluation, is to be continuously evaluating the treatment plan, writing new goals and objectives, and developing targets and future templates accordingly.

Presenting Issue:

Goal and Desired Objectives:

EMDR Preparation Resources, Targets, or Future Templates to Address:
-
-
-
-
-

Presenting Issue:

Goal and Desired Objectives:

EMDR Preparation Resources, Targets, or Future Templates to Address:
-
-
-
-
-

Presenting Issue:

Goal and Desired Objectives:

EMDR Preparation Resources, Targets, or Future Templates to Address:
-
-
-
-
-

Case Conceptualization and Treatment Plan (*continued*)

Presenting Issue:

Goal and Desired Objectives:

EMDR Preparation Resources, Targets, or Future Templates to Address:

-
-
-
-
-

(Use additional copies of this worksheet if needed)

Coping Skills and Emotional Management Plan

POTENTIAL DISTRESS OR SITUATION	SKILL(S) TO USE

(*continued*)

Case Conceptualization and Treatment Plan (*continued*)

Simple Targeting Sequence List for Clinical Tracking

<u>Target Set-Up (Phases 3–7)</u>   <u>Outcome/Plan</u>

1.

2.

3.

4.

5.

6.

7.

8.

Index

CPSIA information can be obtained
at www.ICGtesting.com
Printed in the USA
BVHW071911161020
591230BV00012B/57